INTERNATIONAL RESTAURANTS & BARS

46 Outstanding Restaurants, Cafes, Bars & Discos

目 次

レストラン・各国料理店

カフェ・バール・ブラッセリー

バー・クラブ・ディスコ

CONTENTS

RESTAURANTS

CAFES, TEAROOMS & BRASSERIES

BARS, NIGHTCLUBS & DISCOS

ABBREVIATIONS　略号

A/C――――Air Conditioner　空調機
BC――――Beer Cooler　ビールクーラー
　　　　　Bottle Cooler　ボトルクーラー
Cl――――Closet　押し入れ　物入れ
CR――――Cloakroom　クローク
CTR――――Counter　カウンター
DCT――――Dish up Counter　ディシャップカウンター
DF――――Drinking Fountain　ドリンクディスペンサー
DS――――Duct Space　ダクトスペース
DSP――――Display Space　ディスプレイスペース
DT――――Display Table　ディスプレイテーブル
DW――――Dumb waiter, Lift　ダムウエーター・リフト
EH――――Entrance Hall　エントランスホール
ELEC――――Electrical Room　電気室
ESC――――Escalator　エスカレーター
ELV――――Elevator, Lift　エレベーター
ER――――Employee Room　従業員室
FR――――Fitting Room　フィッティングルーム
GL――――Ground Level　基準地盤面
Hg――――Hanger　ハンガー
LR――――Locker Room　ロッカールーム
MIR――――Mirror　鏡
MECH――――Mechanical Room　機械室
MWC――――Men's Water Closet　男性用便所
PN――――Pantry　パントリー
PS――――Pipe Shaft　パイプシャフト
PT――――Package Table　包装台
R――――Register, Cashier　レジスター・キャッシャー
RV――――Reservoir　受水槽
SC――――Show Case　ショーケース
Sh――――Shelf　棚
SPC――――Sample Case　サンプルケース
SS――――Service Station　サービスステーション
　　　　　Service Area　サービスエリア
St――――Stage　ステージ・陳列台
SW――――Show Window　ショーウインドー
VM――――Vending Machine　自動販売機
WA――――Waiting Area　待合スペース
WBR――――Windbreak Room　風除室
WWC――――Women's Water Closet　女性用便所

CL――――Clear Lacquer　クリアラッカー
EL――――Enamel Lacquer　エナメルラッカー
EP――――Emulsion Paint　エマルションペイント
FB――――Flat Bar　フラットバー
FIX――――Fixed Fitting　はめころし
FL――――Fluorescent Lamp　蛍光灯
HL――――Hair-line Finish　ヘアライン仕上げ
JB――――Jet Burner　ジェットバーナー
JP――――Jet Polish　ジェットポリッシュ
OF――――Oil Finish　オイルフィニッシュ
OP――――Oil Paint　オイルペイント
OS――――Oil Stain　オイルステイン
PB――――Gypsum Board, Plaster Board　石こうボード
PC――――Precast Concrete　プレキャストコンクリート
PL――――Plate　プレート・平板
RC――――Reinforced Concrete　鉄筋コンクリート
S――――Steel Frame　鉄骨
SRC――――Steel Framed Reinforced Concrete
　　　　　鉄骨鉄筋コンクリート
VP――――Vinyl Paint　ビニルペイント
@――――Pitch　ピッチ

本書は1990年から1995年までの季刊・ＷＩＮＤ（WORLD INTERIOR DESIGN）NO.11～NO.32に掲載された作品をセレクトし、構成したものです。作品に関するコメントは、編集者が雑誌に掲載された取材者、または設計者のコメントをもとに新しく文章にまとめています。また、文章中の営業的なデータは雑誌掲載時のものなので、変更されている場合があります。

This book collects projects selected from quarterly magazine WIND(World Interior Design) back numbers published from 1990 through 1995(NO.11～NO.32). All the texts except some of the new projects are summaries by the editor of comments by the reporters and designers.

RESTAURANTS

世界のレストラン

クロスオーバースタイルを導入したフランクフルトのレストラン

スターズ

ドイツ, フランクフルト

Californian Restaurant STARS

Friedrich-Ebert 49, 60308 Frankfurt am Main, Germany
Designer : Jordan mozer & Associates

1．エントランスホールから入り口左側のレジカウンターを見る
2．バーカウンター上部の天井照明器具。ビッグバンにより膨張し続ける宇宙
　をイメージしたフォルム
1．View of the cashier counter from the entrance hall
2．Details of the lighting fixture in the bar area

1

2

●膨張する宇宙のイメージがコンセプト
フランクフルトの国際見本市会場前に位置し、
"リップスティック"の愛称で親しまれている超
高層ビルの地下にこのレストランは２年の歳月を
掛け、計画された。ハイデルベルクでデザインホ
テル＆レストランを経営するオーナーが、サンフ
ランシスコの"サイプレスクラブ"に魅せられ、
ドイツの曇り空の下にもカリフォルニアの太陽が
降り注ぐような食空間を作りたいと考えたのがプ
ロジェクトの始まりであった。民族のるつぼのよ
うなウエストコーストで確立されたカリフォルニ
ア・フリースタイルを、ドイツにも定着させよう
という試みである。設計は"サイプレスクラブ"
を手掛けたシカゴのデザイナー、ジョーダン・モ
ザーが担当することとなった。
空間デザインのコンセプトは、店名の"スターズ"
から天空の星についてのアイデアが追求され、宇
宙は大爆発によって誕生し、常に膨張しつづけて
いるという理論に突き当たった。拡張、成長、発
展を暗示する膨張という基本イメージは、商業空
間のデザインにぴったりであった。そこで、膨張
する空間のイメージがドローイングやモデルで次
第に形作られていった。1950年代から60年代にか
けてのアメリカでは、ありとあらゆる大衆美学が
アメリカとソ連の宇宙開発競争に影響を受け、自
動車のフォルムやネーミング、ＳＦコミックブッ
ク、映画などにもしばしば"宇宙"が登場した。
これらは念入りにリサーチされ、店内のディテー
ルデザインに解釈しなおされて、空間エレメント
として表現されている。

4

STARS

This restaurant opened in a basement level of
a skyscraper called "Lipstick" in front of the
international Frankfurt Messe center. It took
two years to complete this project. The owner
runs a high-end design hotel and a restaurant
in Heidelberg. Attracted by Cypress restaurant
in San Francisco, he decided to build such a
sunny Californian style restaurant in Germany
by the same designer under its cloudy sky. It
was an experiment to transplant Californian
free style, stemmed from so-called a country
of melting pot of races, in Germany.

Design concept is stars, as the name
indicates. The theory of evolveing space and
the big ban influenced the concept making.
Images of expanding, growing, and evolveing
space is evocative for commercial design.
After numerous drawings and model making
to express expanding spatial image, the
interior design was schemed.

Reflecting the space development competition
between the U.S.A. and the U.S.S.R., space
and space ship are favorite symbols of
American pop culture in 50s. and 60s. styles,
and names of automobiles, comic books, films
reflect futuristic space images. Those
nostalgic space age things are carefully
reinterpreted and used in the interior design
elements of this project.

Photos by Henning Queren, text by Hanae Komachi

3．奥のレストラン客席。照明器具をはじめ、すべ
　てのパーツはハンドメードで作られている
4．レストラン客席の仕切りを兼ねたオブジェクト
　のディテール。ねじ曲げられたフォルムがユー
　モラス
3．View of the dining area
4．Details of the art object in the dining area

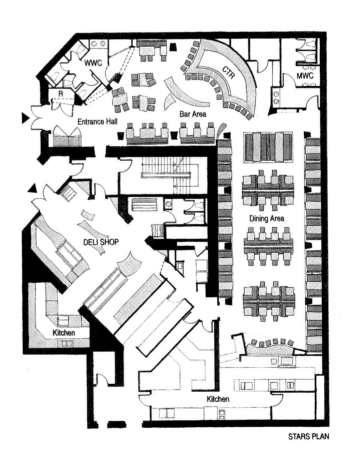

STARS PLAN

分厚い壁の質感を蘇生させたリスボン旧市街のレストラン

コンセンソ

ポルトガル，リスボン

Restaurant CONSENSO

Rua da Academia das 1-1A, 1200 Risbon, Portugal
Designer : Poulo Ludgero de Castro

1．ウエーティングバーのある待合スペース。正面ガラススクリーンの裏側が入り口
2．待合スペースに続く通路に面した客席 "土" の間。土をテーマに草木の繁る自然
　が壁画として描かれている
3．店内最奥に配された客席 "水" の間。壁と天井を覆っているのはプラスター製の
　クラシックな花模様のレリーフ
1．View of the waiting area to the entry
2．Interior view of the dining "La Terra"
3．Interior view of the dining "L' Acqua"

1

2

4

●土・火・水を象徴する三つのダイニング
ヨーロッパ最西端の国・ポルトガルは，かつての大航海時代には海洋国家として繁栄したが，近年では隣のスペインとともに独裁時代が長く続き，西ヨーロッパでは時代に取り残された存在となっていた。しかし，現在では民主化も進み，都市再開発なども動きはじめている。ローマ時代からの長い歴史を持つ首都・リスボンでも，都市再開発計画が進行しているが，その計画の一角に含まれる旧市街バイロー・アルト地区にこのレストランは位置する。
飲食店が数多くあるダウンタウンの，古い居酒屋を改装再生したこの店のデザイン的な特徴は，分厚い壁の質感を生かし，新たな生命を吹き込んだところにある。厚さ70センチメートルにも及ぶ壁の表面や天井は，建物のオリジナルな石積みや細かいレンガが見えるまで削ぎ落とされ，床と同じレベルに配置されたアッパーライトにより，凹凸を鮮やかに浮かび上がらせる。また，三つのダイニングルームはそれぞれに土・火・水というテーマを持ち，テーマにふさわしいモチーフの壁画やレリーフが壁面や天井に配されている。特に最奥の"水"の間の，壁から天井一面にかけての石膏で作られたクラシックなフォルムの花模様のレリーフは，古いパラッツォなどの箱天井を飾った見事な装飾を来客にイメージさせる。

CONSENSO
Situated on the west rim of the Europe, Portugal was once a prosperous oceanic trading country through the age of exploring sailing boats. In the modern era, together with Spain, the country was governed by despotic monarch for a long time, and it got behind other European countries. Recently, however, democratic system is being recovered in Portugal and city development plans are being activated. Lisbon, a city of long history since the Roman Empire, also came out with new development projects. This restaurant is in an area of a old town, on a street full of restaurants and cafes.
Renovated from an old tavern, Consenso looks impressive and vivid with thick walls. The 70cm think ceiling and walls are dismantled to the original old brick and stone masonry. Uplights on the floor level light up ups and downs of wall surfaces. Three dining rooms are designed by themes of earth, fire, and water with the thematic wall paintings and reliefs. Above all, in the "room of water", classical style plaster relief of flower pattern on walls and the ceiling reminds visitors of decorative ceiling of a authentic palazzo.

Photos by Yoichi Horimoto,
text by Masaatsu Fukazawa

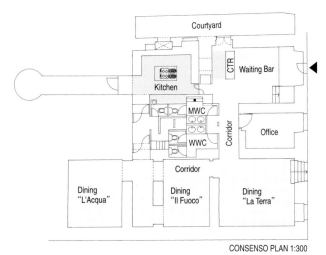

CONSENSO PLAN 1:300

4．店内中央の客席"火"の間。壁面には火をイメージした赤茶色のジグザグ模様が描かれている
5．"土"の間から"火"の間を通して"水"の間を見る。壁・天井は既存のシックイを落とし，建物のオリジナルな石積みの質感を復活させている
4．Interior view of the dining "Il Fuoco"
5．View of the corridor from the "La Terra" to the "L'Acqua"

レストランとクラブを長い通路で結んだトロントの夜の社交場

タブー

カナダ，オンタリオ州，トロント

Restaurant & Nightclub TABOO

2345 Yonge St., Toront, Ontario, Canada
Designer : II BY IV

1．エントランスホールの天井を飾るシャンデリア
2．強烈なレッドカラーで統一されたレストランとバーのエリアを
　　エントランスホール側から見る
1．View of the chandelier in the entrance hall
2．Whole view of the restaurant area from the entrance hall side

1

2

●色彩で区分されたタブーとノア

カナダのトロントは五大湖の一つ、オンタリオ湖に面した港湾都市であり、大陸横断鉄道の要衝として商業の盛んな都市である。周辺人口を合わせると約400万人の大都市であり、対岸はアメリカ合衆国のニューヨーク州である。

このトロントにできたレストラン＆クラブの特徴は、ダイニングエリアとダンシングエリアが離れた位置にあり、それらが長さ38メートルのトンネル状通路で結ばれていることである。入り口側に面したダイニングエリアのカラースキームはゴージャスな赤を基調にし、壁面には金色に輝く百合の花の意匠が配されている。一方、奥のダンシング＆ラウンジエリアは紫を基調にし、メダリオンやゆったりとしたドレープを使って上品で豪華な雰囲気にしている。両者をつなぐアーチ状トンネルは一転してニュートラルなピュアホワイトで塗装され、緩衝空間としての役割を果たしている。

店名のタブーとはトンガ語で禁忌を意味し、その反対語はノア＝自由に行動することである。この店を訪れた来客は、トンネルを通ることによってタブーの世界からノアの境地へと突き抜け、夜の別世界を楽しむことができるのである。

TABOO

Situated by the Lake Ontario, one of Great Lakes in the North America, Toronto is a city of business and the center of railroad transportation, with about 400 million population. The city faces the State of New York .

This project in Toronto characteristically connects a restaurant and a bar by a 38m corridor. Color scheme of dining area is gorgeous red and main motif is an emblem of lily. Club area uses purple as keynote color and decorated with a medallion and rich drapes. The tunnel like corridor, as a kind of buffer zone, has a look of neutral with pure white walls.

The name "taboo" is a word of Tonga language meaning being prohibited by authority or social influence and the antonym is "noa", being free from authenticity. Every night visitors of this club go through a tunnel of taboo and reached the space for noa where they enjoyed themselves in atmosphere of another world.

Photos by David Whitaker,
text by Masaaki Takahashi

3

3．入り口側のレストラン・エリアと奥のディスコ・エリアを結ぶ長さ38メートルの"トンネル"通路
4．ディスコ・エリアのラウンジ側からダンスフロアに面したカウンターバーを見る
5．トンネルの先にあるディスコ・エリア中央のダンスフロア
3．View of the tunnel corridor from the restaurant area side
4．View of the bar counter from the lounge in the disco area
5．View of the dance floor in the disco area

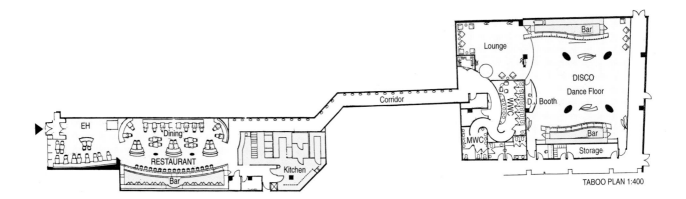

TABOO PLAN 1:400

4

5

クアグリーノズ

イギリス，ロンドン

Spectacle Restaurant QUAGLINO'S

16 Bury Street, St James's, London SW1Y 6AL, England
Designer : Terence Conran, Keith Hobbs, Linzi Coppick

1．道路に面した1階入り口ホールと受付まわり。壁面は販売している小物のショーケースとなっている
2．中地下のピアノバーからダイニングエリア吹き抜け方向を見る
3．地下1階のダイニングエリアから階段を通して見た上部の中地下・ピアノバー客席。
　　互いに見つつ見られつつの関係が成立するスペクタクルな社交場である
1．View of the entrance hall and cashier counter(1F)
2．View of the piano bar to the dining area(MB1F)
3．View of the stairs from the dining area to the piano bar

1

2

●ダンスホールを改装したパノラミック空間
食事とワインと音楽をドラマチックなモダン空間
で楽しめるこのレストランは、ロンドンで"紳士
通り"とよばれ、紳士用品や小物の高級店が並ぶ
ジャーミンストリートからバリーストリートへと
下りていったところにある。1929年に、近くにあ
るセントジェームス宮殿に住んでいた英国皇太子
がパトロン的な存在となってできたこの店は、社
交界の人々がドレスアップして集まり、享楽的な
時を過ごした場所として知られ、リバイバル・オ
ープンした現在でも、ダイアナ妃を始め、各界の
著名人が常連客となっている。
この店のリバイバルを計画したのは、イギリスの
デザイン界でも紳士の中の紳士として知られるテ
レンス・コンラン卿であり、実現までに2年の歳
月と約4億円の費用が投じられた。現在のスペー
スは、地下にあった当時のダンスホールを改装し
たもので、中地下階が新たに作られ、地下の客席
を取り囲む形のギャラリー空間からは、天井にモ
ニュメンタルな人工のスカイライトが輝く広々と
したダイニングエリアをパノラミックに一望する
ことができる。まさに見るため見られるためのド
ラマチックで、スペクタクルなハイソサエティの
ための空間である。

QUAGLINO'S

This restaurant is located on Bury Street and Jermyn Street, which is famous as a street for gentlemen. Customers enjoy dining with nice wine in a dramatic and modern interior. The restaurant was originally patronized by the Prince living in Saint James Palace. Now, after renovation, it is loved by socialites like Prince Diana and other celebrities.

The renovation project was planed by Terrence Conrran, one of he most famous gentlemen of sophisticated taste. Two years and some 400 million yen was invested in this project. Renovated from a basement dance hall, it has a half basement level. The gallery space surrounds the basement level with monumental skylight on the ceiling and it commands a panoramic view of the dining area. It is theatrical and spectacular dining area for the upper class.

Photos by Henning Queren,
text by Hanae Komachi

4．吹き抜けに面した中地下のピアノバー客席から
　見た地下1階のダイニングエリア全景。地下へ
　下りる途中でパノラミックな展望が開ける巧み
　な空間構成である
4．Whole view of the dining area from the
　piano bar side

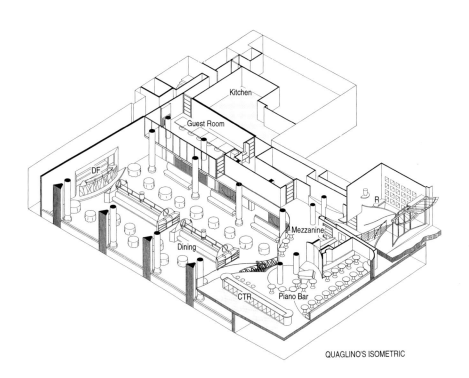

QUAGLINO'S ISOMETRIC

個性的なロンドンのヤングが集まるビアレストラン

ベルゴ・セントラール

イギリス，ロンドン

Beer Restaurant BERGO CENTRAAL

50 Earlham Street, London WC2, England
Designer : Ron Arad, Alison Brooks, Sean Fernandes, Monique van den Hurk

1

1．地下の店内へアプローチする1階入り口のエレベーターホールからブリッジを通して道路方向を見る
2．地下1階エレベーターコアまわりの銅板張り壁面と客席へのアプローチ通路
1．View of the approach bridge from the elevator hall to the street
2．View of the copper wall and corridor to the dining area

●禁欲から解放された近未来修道院

ロンドンのコベントガーデン周辺でも，個性的な
店やファッショナブルな若者が集まるアールハム
ストリートとシェルトンストリートに挟まれた，
レンガ造りの建物の地下にこのビアレストランは
オープンした。この店の売り物は，50種類以上そ
ろっているベルギービールとムール貝とロースト
チキンをメーンとするベルギー料理の数々である。
基本的な店のコンセプトは，ビール醸造工場"ブ
ルワリー"であり，このフィーリングを掴むため
にオーナーはヨーロッパ中を視察し，リサーチを
積み重ねてきたという。
エントランスブリッジから工場用エレベーターで
地下に降りた店内は，ダイニングに至る壁面が鏡
面仕上げの銅板であったり，家具もメタルと木材
のコンビネーションで作られているなど，"サル
ベージ"的なデザインで知られるロン・アラッド
の個性が感じられるが，レンガ貼りの天井や列柱
は既存のものが残され，流用されている。これは，
プロジェクトの予算がないのでローコストで仕上
げなくてはならず，また，工期もごく短期間しか
なかったためである。しかし，ここを訪れる客は，
修道院僧スタイルのウエイターが運んでくるベル
ギービールを飲み，料理を食べているうちに"西
暦2000年のメトロポール修道院"で飲食を楽しむ
"ブレードランナー"の気分に浸れるのである。

BERGO CENTRAAL

Between two fashionable street near Covent
Garden : Earlham Street and Shelton Street,
this restaurant opened in the basement of a
brick building, providing more than fifty kinds
of Belgian beer and Belgian cuisine like roast
chicken. To express the interior design
concept of a beer brewery, the owner took a
research travel around the continent.
Going down by a bridge and an industrial
elevator, you will reach a dining area which
represents designer's salvage art style in
copper mirror palate walls and metal and
wood furniture, etc. Existing brick ceiling and
columns are left, partly because of small
budget and short construction term.
Served by waiters dressed in monk costumes,
customers feel as if they were in a retro
futuristic movie like Blade Runner, over
Belgian drink and food in a atmosphere of
A.D. 2000 monastery.

Photos by Henning Queren,
text by Hanae Komachi

3．アルコーブ風に造られた個室の入り口まわりを
　ダイニングから見る
4．エレベーターコアからのアプローチ通路より見
　たダイニングエリア。メニュー板の表側写真は
　修道院スタイルのウエーター
3．View of the alcove room from the dining
　area
4．View of the dining area from the approach
　corridor

3

4

映画をテーマにしたフロリダ・ディズニーワールド内のレストラン

プラネット・ハリウッド オーランド

アメリカ, フロリダ州, オーランド

Theme Restaurant PLANET HOLLYWOOD Orland
Orland, Florida, USA
Designer : David Rockwell

1

1. ディズニーワールドの湖上に建てられた外観を見る。1階が厨房フロアなので入り口はアプローチ階段を上がった2階レベルに設けられている
2. 2階エントランスホールからSF映画のイメージで作られた円形ゲートを通してダイニング内部客席方向を見る
1. View of the facade and approach stairs on the lake
2. View of the gate from the entrance hall to the dining area

●映画の世界で食事を楽しむ

世界的に有名な映画スターを経営のマイノリティー・パートナーに持ち、アメリカを中心に世界へチェーン展開を図っているレストランの初めての戸建て店舗。アメリカ随一のリゾート地フロリダのディズニーワールド内に立地している。1980年代に新しい娯楽を求める人々へ非日常的空間、非日常的体験の場を提供したテーマパーク。このレストランチェーンは、その延長線上で、映画の都・ハリウッドをテーマとし、夢の世界、虚構の世界、映画の作りだす非日常的雰囲気のなかで、食事やナイトライフを楽しんでもらおうというのが、基本的なコンセプトである。

戸建てであることから実現した球形の外観は、惑星が湖に着陸したイメージから発想されたものであり、高さ33.5メートル、実際に湖の上に建てられている。球形のため構造的な柱のない内部空間は4層に分かれ、1階がキッチン、2・3・4階がダイニングとなっているため、2階レベルに入り口が設けられ、また、2・3階のフロアからは吹き抜けを通して客席全体を見渡せる劇場のようなダイナミックな空間構成である。吹き抜けにはシンボル的な存在である"ダイラマ"（ダイニングエリアにおかれる立体的に作られたハリウッドのイメージ造形物）がフォーカルポイントとして鎮座し、その中央には直径5.4メートルの円形スクリーンが配され、他のモニターとともに映画のシーンを断続的に映し出して、非日常的な雰囲気を盛り上げている。

PLANET HOLLYWOOD Orland

With worldwide famous Hollywood movie stars as managing minority partners, this chained restaurants are now expanding not only in the states but also abroad. This one is the first detached building type in Disney world, Florida, one of he best resorts areas in the U.S.A..

Founded in 1980, Planet Hollywood was established as a thematic amusement restaurant, depended upon themes of Hollywood movies, to offer customers movie-like dramatic and dreaming space to enjoy dining.

Spherical exterior is designed from a imaginary small planet fallen from outer space in a lake. The construction is dynamic. Columns-free interior is divided into four areas. The ground floor is for a kitchen, and from the second floor to

3

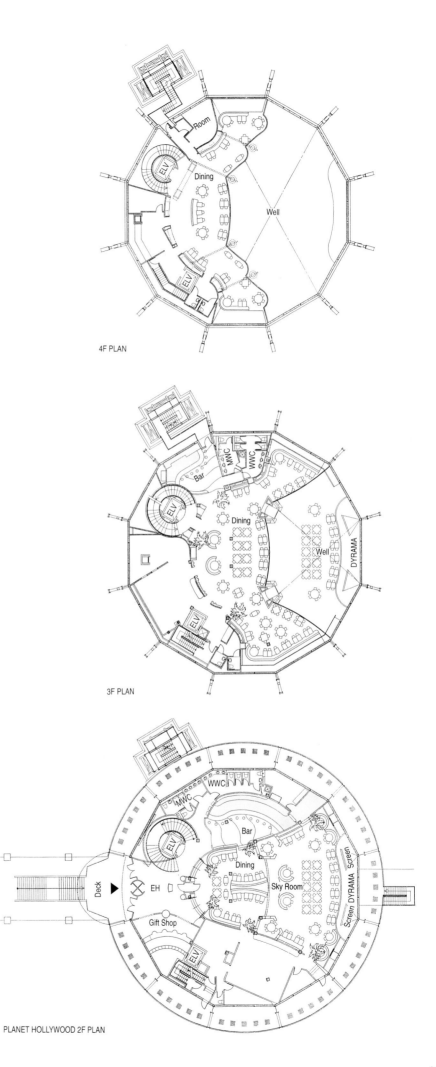

4F PLAN

3F PLAN

PLANET HOLLYWOOD 2F PLAN

the fourth floor is dining area. The entrance is on the second floor for customers to get an overview of the total interior of the third and fourth floor.

In the open ceiling area, there are so-called Dyrama, a symbolic element displaying Hollywood images, as a design focul points. In the center of the space, 5.4m diameter round screen is installed to show movie scenes, together with other monitor screens.

Photos by Paul Warchol, text by Yasuhiko Taguchi

3. 4階客席から吹き抜けを通して2・3階客席を見る。左側壁面に設けられているのが"ダイラマ"とよばれるシンボルゾーンで，中央には巨大な円形スクリーンが配されている

3. View of the "Dyrama"and well from the fourth floor level

アトリウム空間に張り出したロサンゼルスのレストラン

ニコラ
アメリカ，カリフォルニア州，ロサンゼルス

Restaurant NICOLA
601 S. Figueroa Street, Los Angeles, California, USA
Designer : Michael Rotondi

1

1．三和バンク・プラザのアトリウム内部に面して造られたテラスダイニング客席
2．テラスダイニング客席内部。カリフォルニアの陽光を雨・風なしで楽しみながら
　食事をすることができる
1．View of the terrace dining area from the atrium
2．Interior view of the terrace dining area from the entry side

3

●鯨の肋骨に取り囲まれた開放的な空間
ロサンゼルスのダウンタウン商業地に建てられた，日系資本による高層ビル・三和バンクプラザ。その1階アトリウム空間のロケーションを最大限に活用してこのレストランは作られている。ガラス張りの開口部から差し込むカリフォルニアの豊かな自然光，しかも，雨や風の心配はない。アトリウムに張り出した形のテラス席は，アウトドアと変わらぬ自然を楽しみながら食事を楽しむことができるのである。
店のデザインは，この条件を生かすため開放的な作りとされ，アトリウムとの仕切りは巨大な鯨の肋骨を思わせるカーブした木材のピースと座席の背板のみである。この木製の肋骨はインドアの空間にも使われて店内の骨格を形成し，さらに，布とスチールを組み合わせた軽やかな照明器具のデザインが全体のライトでカジュアルな雰囲気を強

調している。

オーナーシェフによるエスニック調のコンテンポラリーなアメリカン・キュイジーヌの魅力と相まって，ロサンゼルスのレストランシーンのなかで話題になっている店の一つである。

NICOLA
A Japanese capital skyscraper Sanwa Bank Plaza is in downtown Los Angels. This restaurant was created in the atrium of the ground floor of the building, making the best of the good location. Californian sunshine comes through the glazed opening. No need to worry about the weather. Terrace seating area can offer an outdoor feeling for customers dining here. Open design with only a huge curved frame like a impressive big whale's rib and wood backrests of chairs. Pieces of the rib are also used for indoor

space to make interior components, and gentle lighting with fabric and steel parts create a warm and comfortable atmosphere. Attractive American cuisine by the owner-chef, this restaurant is a topical spot in Los Angels restaurant scene.

Photos and Text by Takeshi Saito

3．インドアダイニング客席の開口部ガラス窓から見たテラスダイニング客席
4．窓側開口部客席から見たインドアダイニング中央部客席。布地を使ったオブジェと一体化した照明器具のフォルムが軽やかな雰囲気を醸し出している
3．View of the terrace dining through the window from the indoor dining
4．View of the indoor dining from the window side

4

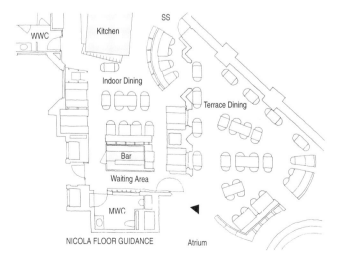

WWC

Kitchen

SS

Indoor Dining

Terrace Dining

Bar

Waiting Area

MWC

NICOLA FLOOR GUIDANCE

Atrium

古い銀行を改装したニューヨークの和食レストラン

ノブ

アメリカ，ニューヨーク州，ニューヨーク

Japanese Restaurant NOBU

105, Hudson Street, New York, USA
Designer : David Rockwell

1．入り口右側客席Aから見た中央客席Bとスシバー。右手の巨大なタイル貼りスクリーンは歌舞伎の舞台をイメージしたもの

Whole view of the dining B and sushi bar from the dining A

●日本の田舎を象徴する三本の白樺

ニューヨーク・マンハッタン島の西側，ハドソン川寄りの古い建物の並ぶトライベッカ地区は，現在，トレンディスポットとして注目を集めており，そこの古い銀行を改装して，この和食レストランは計画された。シェフはロサンゼルスで寿司店"MATSUHISA"を一躍有名にしたノブ・マツヒサ。オーナーの一人が映画スター，ロバート・デ・ニーロということもあって，有名人の社交場ともなっており，ニューヨーカーの話題を集めている。店内のデザインは，シェフの故郷である日本の田舎をテーマとしており，空間をシンボライズするものとして彫刻風にアレンジされた三本の白樺が天井に延び，広がった枝の間から木漏れ日のような明かりが差してくる。中央のスシバーは歌舞伎舞台をイメージしたもので，藍色の薄いタイルの壁は裏からの間接照明により柔らかな光に包まれている。設計を手掛けたデビット・ロックウエルは，ブロードウエイの舞台照明デザイナーであった経験もあり，客にとって心地よく，陰影が強くならないような照明が工夫された。箸の形の椅子，刀の形をした照明器具，掛け軸風の壁掛けなど，日本の伝統色やパターン，素材がインテリアに配され，繊細で，しかもドラマチックな，舞台を思わせる空間となっている。

NOBU

This Japanese restaurant is in Tribecca, a trendy spot of Manhattan, New York. It was renovated from an old bank building. The chef is Matsuhisa Nobu, who owns a legendary famous Sushi restaurant Matsuhisa. Robert de Niro is among the owners of this restaurant and Nobu has become a society for celebrities.

Design concept is from the chef's native place, a rural scene of Japan, which is expressed by sculptural three unprocessed timbers of white birch standing perpendicularly towards the ceiling. The light comes through branches of the trees. The central sushi bar is designed upon a theme of Kabuki stage set, which is covered with light brown tiles and lit up from behind. David Rockwell, the designer of this project, has experience of lighting designer of Broadway and he succeeded in creating comfortable ambience by soft lights. Chop stick-shaped chairs, sword like lamps, wall cover similar to Japanese traditional paintings, and Japanese traditional color scheme and materials are elaborately used and they all make delicate and theatrical environment.

Photos by Paul Worchol,
text by Yasuhiko Taguchi

？　中央客席Bの奥客席と個室客席とを仕切る小枝のスクリーン　View of the screen from the dining B to the private dining

NOBU PLAN 1:300

イギリス料理をベースにしたアムステルダムの無国籍料理店

ベディントンズ

オランダ，アムステルダム

Restaurant BEDDINGTON'S

Roelof Hartsraat 6-8, 1071 Amsterdam, The Netherlands
Designer : Borek Sipek & Niek Zwartjes

1. 客席とガラス開口部を仕切る新たに設けられたスクリーンを客席Bから見る。
　 スクリーンに開けられた小窓により外部からの視線を遮りながら、解放感を演出している
　 View of the dining B and screen from the kitchen side

1

●花びらのエントランスによる変身
　ドイツとベルギーに国境を接し、北海に面したオランダは、干拓により土地を開拓しているため国土の4分の1が海面下にある。ドイツとフランス、イギリスからほぼ等距離に位置するという地理的な条件を生かし、貿易、商業が盛んな国であり、特にチューリップを始めとするフラワー産業は世界をリードしている。首都・アムステルダムの国立博物館を少し南に下がった通りにできたこのレストランは、このような状況を見事に反映している。料理の種類は、自らシェフを務めるイギリス人女性オーナーが持っているイギリス料理のレシピをアレンジしたヨーロッパ風無国籍料理であり、入り口アプローチホールを取り囲む湾曲した壁は、花びらを思わせる優雅なカーブを描いている。こ

のデザインは、既存の建物を改装するにあたり、あまりにもレストランらしくない空間に、オーナーが店にふさわしい味付けをという要望をデザイナーに出し、実現したデザインの一つである。これ以外にも、店の前面を覆うガラス張りの開口部と内部を仕切る、小窓が数多く効果的に開けられたスクリーン状のしっくい壁の新設、洗面台を始めとするトイレの全面的な改装などが行われた。

BEDDINGTON'S
Bordered with Germany and Belgium, the Netherlands opens to the North Sea and the one quarter of the reclaimed land is below the sea level. The Netherlands is easily

accessible from Germany, France, and England at nearly same mileage, so trade and commerce is prospering in the country. Growing tulip is particularly ahead of any countries in the world.
This restaurant on a street on the south side of the National Museum of Amsterdam represents those national character. Based upon a British cuisine by the owner chef, the food of this restaurant is mixed European style. A Curved wall at the entrance gently expresses an image of a flower.
The owner asked a designer to add something expressive to the display the restaurant expressive, for the existing space did not look what restaurant should be. A glazed opening and a partition with small holes, a lime plaster

2

3

4

wall, and renovated rest rooms are the solution.

Photos by Leon Gulikers

2. 厨房前の階段から客席Bを通してエントランスホールと客席A方向を見る
3. オランダらしく花びらをアレンジしたエントランスホールのデザイン
4. 客席Aから見たエントランスホールまわり
2. Whole view of the dining B from the stairs
3. Details of the screen around the entrance hall
4. View of the dining A and entrance hall

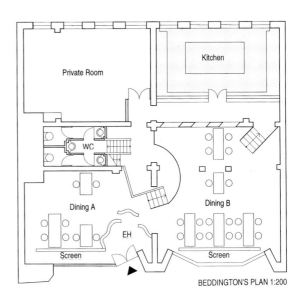

BEDDINGTON'S PLAN 1:200

Private Room

Kitchen

WC

Dining A

Dining B

Screen

EH

Screen

船内の雰囲気を持つアントワープのレストラン

ドックス・カフェ

ベルギー，アントワープ

Restaurant DOCK'S CAFE

7 Jordaens Kaai, Antwerpen, Belgium
Designer : Antonio Pinto

1

1．1階入り口左側の客席Ａから2階へ至る階段を見る。左側に奥のオイスターバーが見える
2．2階から見た階段吹き抜けまわり。客船のインテリアを思わせる空間構成である
1．View of the stairwell from the dining A
2．View of the stairwell from the dining C to the dining A

●モニュメンタルでアンティークな空間

アントワープは，ベルギーではブリュッセルに続く都市であり，北海からスケルデ川を少し遡った河岸にある港湾都市でもある。ヨーロッパ有数の貿易港であり，ダイヤモンド研磨や造船などの工業が盛んである。現在，都市改造計画"リバーサイドシティ"が進行中で，河岸に沿った古い建物は取り壊され，新しくオフィスビル，集合住宅などが次々と建ちはじめた。このレストランは，地区に新しく建てられたビルの1・2階を占めており，大通りを挟んだ向かい側には，保存が決まった今世紀初頭の歴史的造物である長い倉庫が地区の昔の面影をしのばせる。

店名にふさわしく，内部空間はドックに停泊した豪華客船のインテリアを思わせるデザインである。2階ダイニングエリアの吹き抜けに面した部分や階段わきには，羽根の生えた球形のオブジェとそれを支える銅板の柱が配され，その緑青をふいた質感が店内にモニュメンタルでアンティークな雰囲気を漂わせている。バロック，ネオクラシック，アールヌーボーなどが混ざり合った新折衷主義とでもいうべきこのスタイルは，いつかどこかで見たことのある既視感で，来客を船出の気分にさせてくれるのである。

4

DOCK'S CAFE

Antwerp is the second city following the fist one, Brussels and is a bay city close to the North Sea and the River Scheldt. It is one of the best trading ports in Europe and grinding diamonds and the shipbuilding industry is still active. Redevelopment project of Antwerp named River Side City is now proceeding, and old buildings are being dismantled, new office buildings and residential multiple dwelling houses are being constructed one after another. This restaurant occupies the first and the second floor of a newly built building, and a historical landmark warehouse built in the early twenty century is on the opposite side, which has a reminiscence of old street scape of this city.

As the name tells, the interior of this restaurant represents a docked gorgeous ocean liner. Winged sphere objects with copper supports is displayed around the stairwell and stairs. The rusted texture of the objects appear to be authentic and theatrical. Mixed with Baroque, Neo-classicism, and Art Nuveau, the interior has a look of deja-vu feeling.

Photos and text by
Yoichi Horimoto.

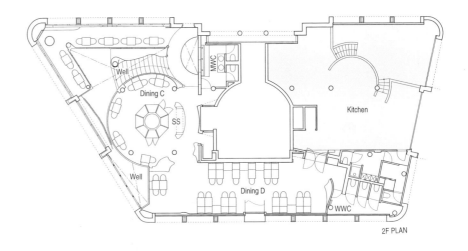

2F PLAN

3．2階の窓側開口部に面したコーナーから客席D方向を見る。緑青仕上げの銅板を使ったオブジェがアンティークなムードを漂わせている
4．2階の客席Dより客席Cのキャビン風客席方向を見る

3．View of the dining C from the window side (2F)
4．View of the dining C from the dining D(2F)

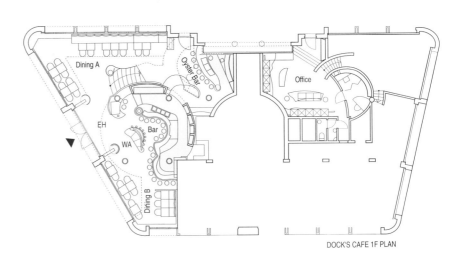

DOCK'S CAFE 1F PLAN

ブリュッセルのネオ・アールデコスタイル・レストラン

グランパレ

ベルギー，ブリュッセル

French Restaurant GRAND PALAIS

16 Rue Grand Cref 1000, Brussel, Belgium
Designer : Raoul Cavadias

1. 店内中央の客席Aからフロアレベルの下がったメーン客席B
   方向を見る。右側は2階の厨房への階段
2. 店内奥を占める中2階客席Cの壁に沿った客席とアールデコ
   風の照明柱
3. メーン客席Bのサービスステーション側に配された燭台のデ
   ィテール
1. View from the dining A to the dining B
2. View of the lighting fixtures and columns in the dining C
3. Details of candlestick in the dining B

2

1

3

4

4．奥の中2階客席Cからメーン客席Bへ下る階段まわり
5．中2階客席Cからメーン客席Bの天井部を見る。
　薄いドレープの布を通して自然光が客席を柔らかく包み込む
4．View of the stairwell from the dining C
5．View from the dining C to the dining B

●アールデコに新しい生命を吹き込んだ空間
ベルギーは，1830年にオランダから独立した小国で石炭資源に恵まれ，鉄鋼・機械を始めとする重工業が盛んである。歴史的なデザインの流れから見ると，19世紀末のアールヌーボー時代にその中心的存在であったヴィクトール・オルタの活躍の場であり，その後，1920年代にパリから輸入されたアールデコも，短期間に市民権を得，現在も多くの作品が残されている。アールデコは飽きの来ない"近代的なクラシックデザイン"として評価され，現在でも愛好者が多い。
この高級フランス料理店は，アールデコに新しい生命を吹き込んだネオ・アールデコともいうべきスタイルを持ち，レストランの多い首都・ブリュッセルでも評判の店である。入り口側から順次，奥へと続く四つのレベル差のある客席は，モダンなアールデコ感覚でまとめられ，随所に配されたグリーンが空間を生き生きとしたものにしている。また，ブリュッセルの暗く，長い冬を少しでも明るく過ごすために，奥部分の天井には採光のために天窓が設けられ，白い布を通してソフトな自然光が空間を包み込んでいる。

GRAND PALAIS

Since it won its independence from the Netherlands in 1930, Belgium has been prospering in heavy industry like steel and machinery, with the advantage of rich coal production. In terms of design history, at the end of the last century Belgium produced Victor Horta, one of the most important figure of Art Nouveau movement and the city also zealously imported Art Deco style from Paris in 1920s. They became modern classic standard style and still loved by many people. This classy French restaurant in Brussel, decorated by a kind of Neo-Art Deco style, revitalizing art deco, became popular. There are four areas with gradual rises from the entrance to the back. Modern version of Art Nouveau is realized in the interior with the accents of plants to give lively atmosphere. Skylights lets the natural light in and helps customers to spend time here forgetting long gloomy winter. The natural light comes through roof light windows in the back and it fills the interior with soft brightness.

Photos and text by Yoichi Horimoto.

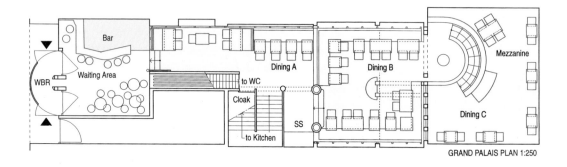

GRAND PALAIS PLAN 1:250

ベニハナ

イギリス，ロンドン

Steak House BENIHANA

73-79 Kings Road, London, England
Designer : Kiyofumi Okamoto, Takenaka(UK)Ltd.

1

1．ステージ風の階段から見たメーン客席。間接照明を内蔵した
　左側アート壁面のエッジは世界の海岸線をトレースしたもの
2．金屏風をイメージした1階エントランスから地下に至る階段
　ホールの壁面デザイン
3．カクテルラウンジからステージ風の広い階段スペースを見る。
　階段頂部左側にはギャラリー的なアプローチ通路が見える

1．View of the dry pond and main dining from the stairs
2．View of the stairwell from the entry
3．View from the cocktail lounge to the stairs

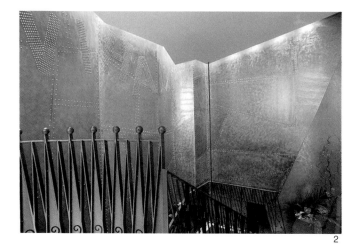

●地下の大空間が一挙に広がる劇的な構成
ロンドンのキングスロードは、かつてはパンク文化の発祥の地であり、現在でも、最もロンドンらしいストリートの一つである。ここに、アクション豊かなパフォーマンスでアメリカを席巻した、ロッキー青木が率いるステーキレストランがヨーロッパ第二号店を出店した。計画に当たっての最大の問題点は、地下空間にアプローチする1階ファサードの間口が2メートルしかないことであった。そのために、入り口からの階段部分の垂直と水平の視点の動きが何度もシミュレーションされ、途中の中地下レベルに客席を一望できるギャラリー的な通路が設けられたり、随所に謎解きのような仕掛けが散りばめられるといった具合に、エンターテインメントの要素が高められている。また、この店は日本レストランであるが、デザインのコンセプトは従来の東洋趣味に頼ることなく、現代の日本人である設計者から見た伝統的な日本、異邦人としての日本人から見たイギリス的、ヨーロッパ的なものが直観的に取り入れられた。この結果、生じるある種のぎこちなさ、違和感、ひそかなギャップこそが、現代日本を表出しているというのが設計者の主張である。

BENIHANA

Kings Road was once a mecca of punk culture, and it is still a hive of London pop culture. Rocky Aoki, an owner of American-based chained restaurants famous for its showy performance in front of customers. This project is the second one as his first step to European market. The problem in designing this was the 2m wide entrance approaching to the basement level. To make this narrow approach smoothly, designers repeatedly experimented vertical and horizontal eye levels by simulation tests. As a result, half basement level gallery was made to look over the basement. Besides, there are some devices to add variety to the interior to entertain customers. Although the food is Japanese, the design concept is not stereotypical Orientalism and the design is modernized Japanese style using British and European elements, from which a kind of cacophony arises. It is designers' intention to represent contemporary chaotic situation in Japan.

Photos by Henning Queren,
text by Hanae Komachi

4. カクテルラウンジから見たメーンダイニング全景。天井の排気フードも視覚的なインパクトを与えるようにシャープにデザインされている
4. Whole view of the main dining from the cocktail lounge

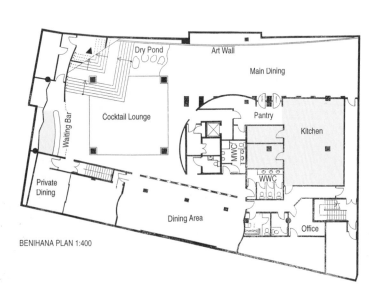

BENIHANA PLAN 1:400

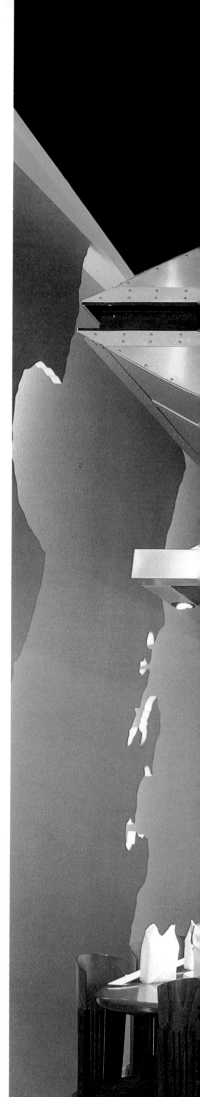

4

過剰なフォルムを持つシカゴのイタリアンレストラン

ビベーレ

アメリカ, イリノイ州, シカゴ

Italian Restaurant VIVERE

71 W.Monroe St., Chicago, Illinois, USA
Designer : Jordan Mozer & Associates

1．1階エントランスホール側から細長い客席Aを通して奥の客席B方向を見る
2．1階奥の客席B全景。ラセンをテーマにしたオブジェ的な照明器具が4隅と
天井に配されて空間を過剰なまでに装飾している
1．View from the entrance hall to the dining A
2．Whole view of the dining B from the dining A

2

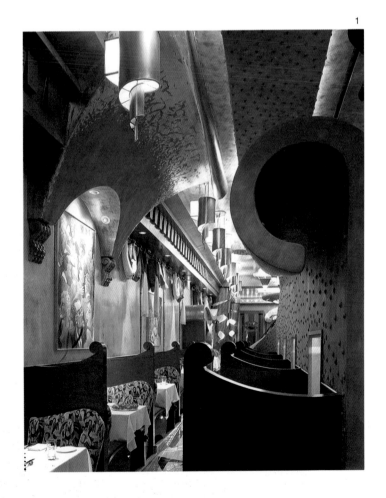

1

●ラセンをモチーフとしたバロック的空間
五大湖の一つ、ミシガン湖に面したアメリカ中北部
最大の都市・シカゴのダウンタウンにあるこのイタ
リアンレストンは、三代にわたってレストランを営
むイタリア人一家が経営する、三つのレストランが
複合した"イタリアンビレッジ"の一部を改装した
ものである。以前は"フィレンツェ風の部屋"と呼
ばれていた部分をリニューアルするに際して、シカ
ゴを本拠地に世界的な活動を展開しているジョーダ
ン・モザーにデザインが依頼された。
使い古されてはいるが、重厚でシンボリックな

力を感じさせた既存の空間イメージを生かしな
がら、新しい店に生まれ変わらせるために採ら
れたのが、独自の手作り手法であった。照明器
具、家具などすべてがハンドメイドのオリジナ
ルであり、モザーはデザインするだけでなく自
らメタルを加工し、ガラスを吹くアルチザンで
もある。デザインのモチーフには、連綿と続い
たイタリア人一家三世代の象徴として "ラセン"
が選ばれ、現代版バロックともいうべき彫刻的
なボリュームとリズム、色使いが、過剰とも言
える独特の空間を作り出している。

VIVERE
Chicago is the third largest city in the U.S.A.
on Lake Michigan. This restaurant is in down
town Chicago where the three-generation
owner family runs an Italian restaurant
complex named Italian Village. Among them is
the one called Florentine room, which was
renovated by Jordan Mozer, a Chicago-based
international interior designer.
Keeping existing old and dignified images,
Mozar totally changed the atmosphere by his
hand-made artful methodology. He made

every single details, including lamps and
furniture. He is also a craftsman who can cast
metals, blow glass on his own.
The design motif is spiral as a symbol of
evolveing generation. Sculptural forms, rich
color scheme, sense of volume, all these
create unique modern Baroque style.

Photos by David Clifton,
text by Masaaki Takahashi

3．2階客席への階段降り口から１階客席Aのボトルキャビネットを見る
View of the dining A from the dining C through the stairs

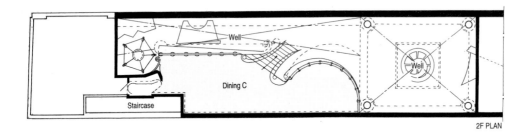

2F PLAN

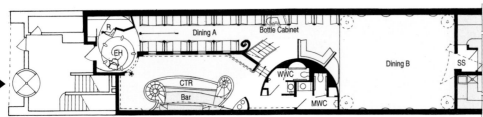

VIVERE 1F PLAN

文化のメルティング・ポットを体現したトロントのレストラン

アクロバット

カナダ，オンタリオ州，トロント

Restaurant ACROBAT

1221 Bay Street, Tront, Ontario, Canada
Designer : Alexandre and Gregory Gatserelia

1．店内右側を占めるカウンターバー席を客席Aから見る。カウンターバック上部の照明器具は廃ビンを使用　View from the dining A to the bar counter

2

●一本の梁から発想された店づくりのテーマ

カナダのトロントは、ルーツは1615年に遡ることができ、市としても150年の長い歴史を持つ。アメリカと国境を接し、人口の集中しているカナダの南部に位置し、人種構成も多種多様である。カナダは1970年代に最も多くのボートピープル（難民）を受け入れた国であり、アメリカとともに人種のルツボといわれているが、アメリカがサラダボウルとすれば、カナダはモザイクに例えられる。つまり、モザイクの一片一片が独立しているのである。トロントにできたこのレストランは、デザインを手掛けたガツェレリア兄弟の両親がグルジア人とレバノン人であり、パリとベイルートで教育を受けた。また、店内のカウンターバックに配されたカラフルなボトルのガラススクリーンもモザイク風で、トロントの置かれた状況を見事に象徴している。

店内デザインは、既存空間にあった一本の大きな構造梁から発想され、ここからウイットのあるエスカペイド（遊び、脱線）として、空中を自由に飛び跳ねるアクロバットがテーマとして採用された。無数の色とシンボルが溢れる空間は、遊園地かサーカスを想起させる賑やかさで、まさにアクロバット曲芸の場にふさわしい。

ACROBAT
Bordered with the U.S.A., Toronto has more than 380 year history, and 150 year as a city. It is located in the south part of Canada where the population is dense. City of multi culture.
As the U.S.A. is called a salad of races, Canada is called a mosaic of races. The difference is that each piece of a mosaic is independent and indispensible. Gatserelia brothers, the designers of this project represents city's character. They are born to a couple of Gerogian and Lebanese, and educated in Beirut and Paris, and now based on Toronto. A decorative colorful bottle screen behind a bar counter might represent mosaic nation of Canada.
Gatserelias came across the idea of the interior design when they work on a long existing beam crossing the inside of the space. They create something acrobatic as an element of escapade. Like an acrobatic performer jumping and playing around freely, the interior of this restaurant, like a circus, is full of surprise and entertainment. Marriage of vivid and playful colors and symbolic design elements are quite becoming to the name of Acrobat.

Photos by Rico Bella,
text by Masaaki Takahashi

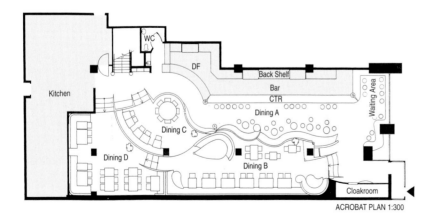

ACROBAT PLAN 1:300

2．厨房出入り口から客席Cを通してエントランス方向を見る
3．店内最奥の客席Dより客席Cを通して見たカウンターバー客席。中央の梁上部にはアクロバットを演ずる人形がいる

2．View of the dining C from the kitchen side
3．View from the dining D to the dining C and bar counter

ハリウッドのアトラクションモール内にできたテーマ・レストラン

ウィザーズ・アト・MCA・シティウォーク

アメリカ, カリフォルニア州, ハリウッド

Theme Restaurant WIZARDZ at MCA Citywalk

Universal City, Hollywood, California, USA
Architect : Hirata Architect
Graphics & Interior Designer : Communication Arts

1

● "魔法" をテーマとしたデザインコンセプト
映画産業の中心地・アメリカのハリウッドは、マル
チメディア時代を制する膨大なソフトのストックを
持っていることで、全世界から熱い視線を集めてい
る。ここにある広大なユニバーサル・スタジオを使
って作られた、映画をテーマとしたテーマ・パーク
も、ディズニーランドやディズニーワールドと並ん
で人気を博し、多くの人々を集めているが、これも
映画の持つ魅力のたまものであろう。
MCAシティウォークは、ユニバーサル・スタジオ内
に新しく作られたアトラクションモールで、その通
りのなかにこのテーマ・レストランはある。テーマ
は "魔法" であり、吹き抜けのある2階のバー&ラ
ウンジ中央には、魔法使い（ウィザード）のかぶる
トンガリ帽子の形をした巨大なバーカウンターが配
されている。それを取り巻く空間は、まさにネオン
ライトの洪水、天井に広がるネオンのリングは惑星
の軌道を表し、その輝きが店内を宇宙空間の雰囲気
にし、客を楽しませる。奥にはレーザーなどを使っ
たライティング・ショーの舞台があり、それを見物
しながら飲食のできる客席が用意されている。

WIZARDZ at MCA Citywalk

Hollywood is now, needless to say, not only
the midmost point of movie industry but also a
heart of multimedia business with its vast soft
stock and other resources. Many people keen
on visiting thematic park like one linked with
Universal studio, as well as Disneyland and
Disneyworld. No other thing like movie can
attract people so easily.
MCA Citywalk is an attraction mall in
Universal studio and a restaurant WIZARDZ is
in there. A keyword of design concept is
magic. A big pointed cap shaped bar counter
is in the center of bar lounge on the second
floor with a big void. And around it, there is
flood of neon lights. A circled neon represents
an orbit and it creates an atmosphere of outer
space. On the third floor, customer enjoy
dining, seeing laser lighting show.

Photos by Gray Crawford,
text by Ina Kikugawa

1．ストリートの両側から内部の華やかなネオンが良く見えるファサードのデザイン
2．2階バーラウンジに配されたカウンター上部のネオンオブジェ。左右のガラス壁
　　面に映り込んだ虚像が効果を増幅する
1．View of the facade from the Citywalk street
2．View of the counter and neon art in the bar lounge(2F)

3

4

5

6

3．2階バーラウンジを3階のエレベーター前ラウンジから見る
4．入り口側から見た2階のダイニングシアター客席とステージ
5．1階キャラクターグッズショップの入り口まわりを見る
6．ダイニングシアターのステージで演じられるレーザーを使った光のショー

3．View of the second floor bar lounge from the third floor lounge
4．View of the dining theater from the entry side(2F)
5．Entrance view of the character goods shop(1F)
6．View of the lighting show in the dining theater

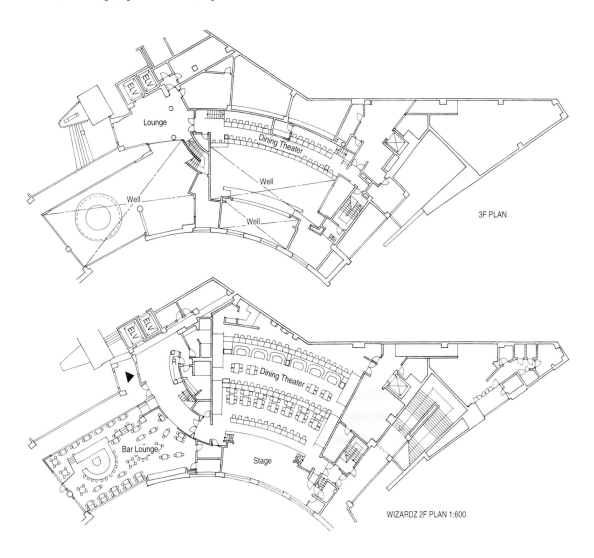

Lounge

Dining Theater

Well

Well

Well

3F PLAN

ELV

Bar Lounge

Dining Theater

Stage

WIZARDZ 2F PLAN 1:600

劇場を再生したマドリッドのレストラン＆バー

テアトリッツ
スペイン，マドリード

Restaurant & Bar TEATRIZ
Hermosilla 15, Madrid, Spain
Designer : Philippe Starck

1

1．ウエーティングコーナーからメーン客席へ至る細い通路。この先に予期せぬ広い空間
　が広がる巧みな導入の演出
2．劇場の桟敷席部分をそのまま生かした2階のメンバーズクラブ客席をバー側から見る。
　正面奥のカーテンを一部あけて向こう側の吹き抜け大空間を垣間見せている
3．1階奥のステージから見たメーン客席全景。劇場の吹き抜けにビロードのカーテンを
　吊り下げることによって，大空間を効果的に蘇生させている
1．View of the approach corridor from the waiting area to the main dining(1F)
2．View from the member's club to the well(2F)
3．View of the main dining from the stage(1F)

2

4

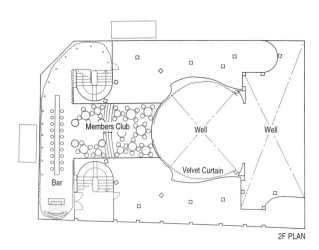

2F PLAN

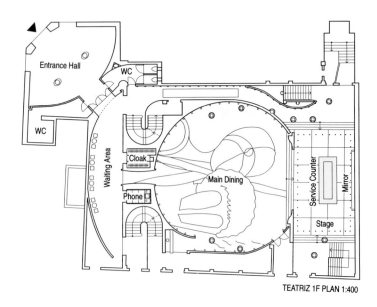

TEATRIZ 1F PLAN 1:400

●劇場の大空間を生かした巧みなデザイン

長く続いたフランコ独裁時代から脱却し、西側ヨーロッパの一員として経済成長に懸命のスペイン。その首都・マドリードにできたこのレストラン＆バーは、1900年代の初めに建てられた古い劇場を改装したものである。コロン広場から少し離れた山の手地区にあるこの建物は、昔の面影を残したまま、1階がレストラン、2階がメンバーズクラブ、地下1階がサロン風バーと小さなディスコへとリニューアルされた。

入り口からエントランスホールを抜けた左側が、劇場時代はホワイエだった広々としたウエーティングで、その中央部からコリドーを通して向こう側にレストランの大空間が広がる。さらにその奥には劇場時代そのままにステージが残され、内部照明により全体が発光して見えるオニックス製の巨大なサービスカウンターが目に飛び込んでくる。パースペクティブを十分に計算し尽くしたドラマティックな空間構成であり、いかにもスタルクらしい巧みなデザインである。また、1階レストランの客席は上部が円形に吹き抜けており、周囲を取り巻く最上部の天井桟敷から下部へ向けて、長い長いブルーグレーのドレープ・カーテンが吊り下げられ、ヒダを浮き上がらせるスポットライトにより、空間の高さを強調している。

TEATRIZ

Freed from Franco despotic government, Spain has endeavored to accelerate economic growth as a potential member of EU.

This restaurant and bar in Madrid is a renovation project on an old theater built in early 1900s. It is located in uptown with old existing exterior. The first floor is a restaurant and the second floor is a member's club, and the basement is bar lounge and disco.

Left hand side of the entrance used to be a foyer and now it is a spacious waiting room. The central corridor of the room leads to a dining area where lies an onyx made big counter with built-in light gleams. Dynamic perspective of the spectacular interior design is effectively planned. A around void on the ceiling of the dining room of the first floor. A long blue draped curtain goes along the void hanging from the top to emphasize a sense of the height.

Photos by Yoichi Horimoto,
text by Masaatsu Fukazawa

4．2階メンバーズクラブのバーカウンターを入り口側から見る
5．劇場の舞台上に設けられたオニックス製のサービスカウンター。ホリゾントには巨大なミラーが立てかけられている
4．Whole view of the bar counter in the member's club(2F)
5．View of the service counter on the stage (1F)

騎士の時代を再現したエッセンのレストランホテル

ミントロープスブルク

ドイツ，エッセン

Restaurant Hotel MINTROPSBURG
Schwargens teimweg 81, Essen, Germany
Designer : Dirk Obliers

1

1．外部へ半円形に張り出したレストラン奥の客席。ハイバックチェアの
　背は騎士の楯をイメージさせる
2．レストラン中央部のスクリーンに囲まれた客席とボトルキャビネット
1．View from the dining area to the garden
2．View of the center seatings and bottle cabinet in the dining area

3

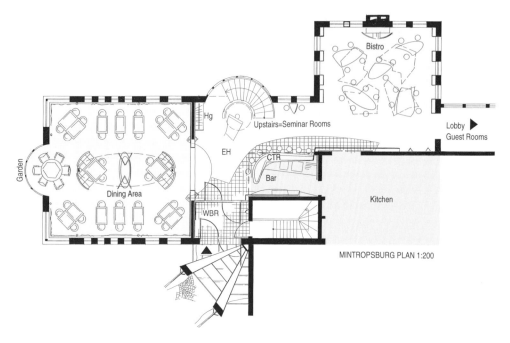

MINTROPSBURG PLAN 1:200

ルール地方はドイツの北西部にあり、ヨーロッパ
でも有数の工業地帯である。その中心都市・エッ
センの郊外、緑に恵まれた丘の上にこのレストラ
ンホテルはある。飲食棟の改装に当たり、デザイ
ンのテーマには"騎士の時代"が選ばれた。これ
は、隣のバイエルン州には19世紀に領主・ルード
ヴィヒII世が狂ったように建設した城が数多く残
され、現在では観光の目玉となっていることと、
設計を手掛けたディルク・オブリールスが、ルー
ドヴィヒII世がパトロンとなっていたワーグナー
の崇拝者であることと無関係ではないだろう。
楯をイメージした椅子の背、槍の形をしたブラケ
ット照明器具などのインテリアデザインはいうま
でもなく、レターヘッドや食器に至る小物までト
ータルにデザインされた店内は、中世の城内をモ
ダンに再構成している。空間のもう一つの特色は
照明にある。騎士の時代の城内は暗かったであろ
う。明るすぎる照明は中世の雰囲気を感じさせな
い。このため、照度を押さえ気味ながら、メリハ
リのきいた、空間にふさわしいライティング手法
が導入された。

MINTROPSBURG

Ruhr, in the northwest part of Germany, one
of the eminent industrial districts in Europe
and the central city in Essen. This hotel
stands on a hill with forests in a suburb of the
city. Renovation design concept for a
restaurant is "the age of kinights", it might has
something to do with Bavarian king Ludwig II,
a patron of Richard Wagner, who zealously
continued to built several castles. Dirk Obliers,
a designer of this project seemed to adore
Wagner's opera in which a number of knights
appear.

Back rests of chairs look like shields, wall
sconces are like spears. From the letter head
to tableware and other small goods in this
hotel are designed upon images of a medieval
age castle. Not too dark but modestly
subdued, the lighting design is successful,
which evokes an theatrical atmosphere of the
Middle Ages.

Text by Masaaki Takahashi

3．入り口右側のバーからエントランスホールを通
　して左側レストラン方向を見る
4．バー側から見た右奥のビストロ・コーナー。壁
　面ブラケットが槍の形をしている
5．腰部分が鎧のような構造を持つバーのカウンター
3．View from the bar area to the dining area
　through the entrance hall
4．Whole view of the bistro area from the bar
　side
5．Details of the counter in the bar area

4

5

バルセロナのアメリカン・ダイナー風レストラン

セルビシオ・ウィルソン

スペイン，バルセロナ

American Diner SERVICIO WILSON

Quatre Camins 72, Barcelona, Spain
Designer : Inigo Correa y Federico Turull

1

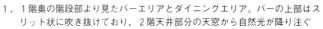

1．1階奥の階段部より見たバーエリアとダイニングエリア。バーの上部はスリット状に吹き抜けており、2階天井部分の天窓から自然光が降り注ぐ
2．道路側から見た外観夜景。モデルニスモ・スタイルの建築をそのまま残している
3．1階の入り口側から見たダイニングエリア全景
1．View of the dining area and bar from the stairs side(1F)
2．Night view of the facade from the street side
3．Whole view of the dining area from the entry side(1F)

2

3

4．2階奥から見たダイニングエリア。窓側の広い開口部と天井のスリット状天窓により店内はカジュアルで明るい雰囲気になっている
View of the dining area and slit well(2F)

2F PLAN

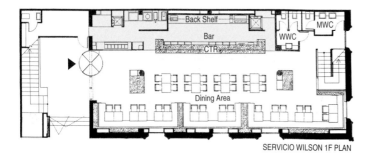

SERVICIO WILSON 1F PLAN

● モデルニスモ様式の住宅を現代に蘇らせる

バルセロナは、首都・マドリードと並ぶスペインの二大都市であるが、また、独自の文化、風土を持つことでも知られている。建築デザインの面では、ガウディが有名であり、かれに代表される19世紀末の建築様式は"モデルニスモ"とよばれ、有機的な曲線による独特の装飾が特徴である。バルセロナの山の手に属し、私立学校や高級住宅の多い閑静な場所にあるこのレストランは、100年近く経ったモデルニスモ・スタイルの住宅を改装し、現代に蘇らせたものでる。
アメリカで長く暮らしていたオーナーの要望は、アメリカン・ダイナーのイメージをモデルニスモ・スタイルと大胆に組み合わせ、若いビジネスマンが気軽に海外のクライアントとの接待にも使えるようなコスモポリタンな店にすることであった。まず、古い建物の魅力を生かすため、道路側正面にあった入り口が移動され、左端側面に新しく作り直された。次に小さな部屋に分かれていた内部空間は、仕切りが取り払われて見通しのよい大空間にされ、1階カウンター席の上部にはトップライトを持つスリット状の吹き抜けが設けられた。この結果、1、2階の客席は視覚的に連結され、また、道路側の開口部と奥のトップライトの両側から自然光が差し込むので、客は快適で、しかも上品な雰囲気の中で食事を楽しむことができるのである。

SERVICIO WILSON

Different from Madrid the capital of Spanish government, Barcelona is the center of Catalan culture, which produced a number of geneniuses such as Gaudi. And Modernismo (Modernism) was hatched in the 19th century here. Organic curve lines and decoration is characteristic in Modernism architecture represented by Gaudi. This restaurant was renovated from a 100 years old residential building of Modernism style.

The owner, who lived in the U.S.A. for a long time, combined an American diner style and Spanish Modernismo, to create cosmopolitan environment for young business people to dine and talk with their foreign clients. To keep the existing parts of the building, the entrance on the road side has moved to the left of the building. Small rooms of the interior has changed into one space, wiping out columns. Above a counter on the first floor, there is a slit opening with skylight. So, the first and second floor is visually integrated and natural light comes in from a road side opening and the skylight. Dining here in comfort and gentle atmosphere soothes customers mind.

Photos by Ferran Freixa, Rafael Vargas,
text by Kyoko Asakura

大草原に立つハンガリーのレストラン

グヤチャールダ

ハンガリー，バラトンセントジェルジュ

Restaurant GULYA CSÁRDA

Balaton Szentgyörgy, Hungary
Architect : Gábor Sánta

1．大草原に立つ外観を見る。特異な外観はハンガリー遊牧民の野営テントのデザインをアレンジしたもの　View of the facade standing on the plain

●大地に生きるオーガニック・アーキテクチュア

東欧の中央に位置するハンガリーは、ヨーロッパで唯一のアジア系遊牧民・マジャール人の国であり、独自の文化を持っていることで知られている。その文化の表出の一つが、建築におけるオーガニック・アーキテクチュアであり、大地に根差した有機的なフォルムは人々を引きつける魅力に満ちている。

ハンガリー遊牧民の野営テントの形態を基にしたこのレストランは、ユーゴスラビアとの国境に近いバラトン湖のほとりにあり、背後は大平原である。壁面がゆるやかに湾曲し、排煙用の穴のある頂部で合わされる構造は、古い塔などの建築に使われていたものであり、初期のコンセプトでは、円形と方形による求心的な構造の四つのドームがコーナーに広がり、中央にタワーのあるデッキを持ち上げるという構想であった。その後、計画を引き継いだ若い建築家、ガーボル・シャンタがタワーの基部に暖炉を配し、タワーを火炎魔のトーテムポールとして象徴化した。四つのコーナードーム頂部には、煙抜きの替わりにトップライトが設けられ、自然の最大の恵みである自然光が室内へ豊かに降り注いでいる。

GULYA CSÁRDA

Situated in the core of Eastern Europe, Hungary has mainly Magyar population, whose language is Uralic. It has unique Asian culture. Organic architecture is stemmed from its mother earth of Magyar, attracting people's attention.

Based upon a configuration of Hungarian nomadic tents, this restaurant is on the Lake Balaton near the border with Yugoslavia. The backdrop is plain. Walls curve gently and get together above a smoke duct, and the construction is taken from that of old towers. According to the design concept of the early stage, it was planned to have four domes in around or square shapes with the central tower supported by a deck. Later, however, a young architect Gabor Santa was commissioned the deign and he made a fireplace at the bottom of the tower. Four tops of each domes has totem poles instead of smoke ducts, which let the natural light in.

Photos and text by Kiyo Matsumoto

2．天井にドームを持つ客席Aを入り口側から見る
3．四角錐のようなフォルムのドーム天井と排煙窓をトップライトに置き換えた頂部のディテール
2．View of the dining A from the entry side
3．Details of the dome and top light

3

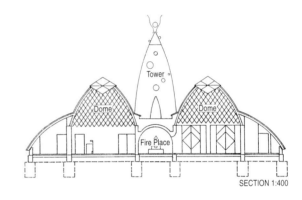

SECTION 1:400

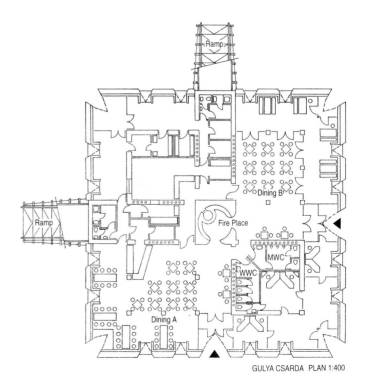

GULYA CSARDA PLAN 1:400

1

竹を使った上海のカントニーズレストラン

愚斎閣

中国，上海

Chinese Restaurant SHENG VILLA

Tsuniru 300, Shanghai, China
Designer : Edward Suzuki Arch.

1．竹のスクリーンを道路との間に設けたファサード
2．メーンダイニング席中央から道路側開口部を見る
3．入り口側から見たメーンダイニング席全景
1．View of the facade from the street
2．View from the main dining to the street side
3．Whole view of the main dining from the entry side

2

3

４．メーンダイニング席から見たエントランスホールと待合スペース　View of the entrance hall and waiting area from the main dining

●中国のイメージを "竹" に象徴させる

急激な経済成長により、中国の沿海部にある大都市の変貌は著しい。なかでも上海は建設ブームで、日々、新しいビルが立ち上がり、しばらく見ないと街の様子が変わってしまうほどの急ピッチさである。道路に面したビルの１階にあるこの広東料理店は、東京の千駄ヶ谷にある "新亜飯店" の姉妹店で、経営者も同じであり、設計デザインも同じ建築家が手掛けている。

東京の店と同じく、中国＝竹というイメージでデザインは進められたが、意外なところに落とし穴があった。上海では、竹を入手するのが非常に困難であったのだ。必要な太さと長さ、樹種の竹は上海近辺で取れず、輸送手段が鉄道しかないため産地から送るのも大変であった。やっと工事が始まったものの、職人の技術が低く、人夫のレベルでしかないため日数が延び、３カ月の予定が半年に延びて、工事が終わったときには仕上がりの床に３センチメートルの埃が積み重なっていたほどである。しかし、シンプルだが竹をうまく使いこなしたモダンなデザインも相まって、このレストランは多くの来客を集めている。

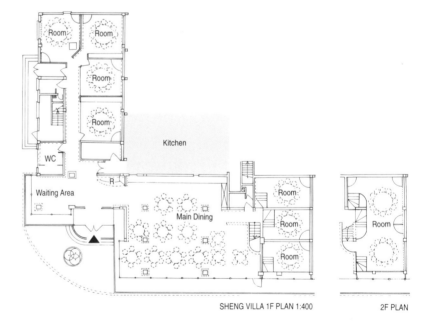

SHENG VILLA 1F PLAN 1:400   2F PLAN

SHENG VILLA

With the rapid economical growth, big cities on sea side of the mainland China show drastic change. It is shifting very first beyond our expectation. This Cantonese restaurant on a floor of a road side building is a sister restaurant of Sina-hanten in Sendagaya, Tokyo designed and managed by the same people. Following the same design concept for previous project in Tokyo, China=bamboo, designers unexpectedly had to change their ways, for it was quite hard to acquire bamboos even in Shanghai. Appropriate size bamboos for this project do not grow near Shanghai, so suitable size bamboos had to be conveyed from other places where railroad is the only transportation system. Even after the project started, the construction period was prolonged months by immature and unskilled builders. Three month schedule resulted in six months and 3cm think dust covered the floor after the project was completed. Simple but modern with bamboo design elements, this restaurants attracts a number of customers.

Photos and text by Edward Suzuki

CAFES & BRASSERIES

世界のカフェ＆ブラッセリー

シンボリックなアイコンで彩られたフィレンツェ郊外のバール

マダレーナ

イタリア，プラト

Bar MADDALENA

Piazza S.Agostino 2, Prato, Italy
Designer : KING KONG Stefano Giovannoni and Guido Venturini

1

1．入り口より奥へバールカウンターを見る。天井にプロジェクターで映し出された店名ロゴと人の顔は揺れ動く
2．入り口右側の開口部に面した"恋人たちの部屋"。壁面のイラストは愛と死を表現
3．店内右奥の細長い"ブルーの部屋"。眼のような二つの孔が開いたオブジェスクリーンは回転する

1．View of the bar counter and passage from the entry
2．View of the Sweetheart room from the entry side
3．View of the Blue room and revolving screen

2

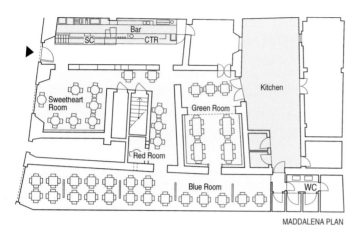

MADDALENA PLAN

4．バールから中央通路を通って"ブルーの部屋"へ行く途中にある赤の部屋
5．厨房に面した"グリーンの部屋"から隣の"ブルーの部屋"方向を見る
4．View from the center corridor to the red room
5．View from the green room to the blue room

4

5

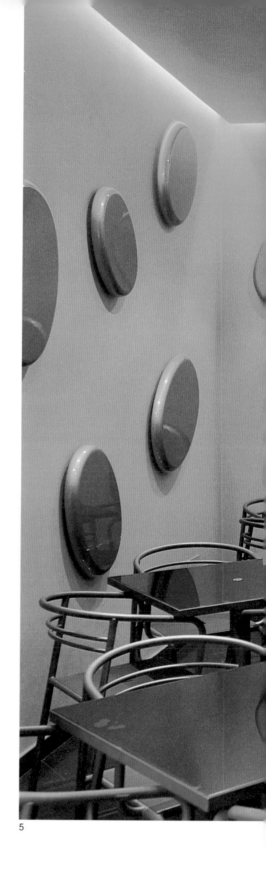

●アリス・ワンダーランドのトリップ感覚
このファンタスティックなバールは，フィレンツェ
の北西20kmに位置する街・プラトにつくられた。
設計を手掛けたのは，1980年代前半，フィレンツ
ェを中心に起こったデザイン・ムーブメント"ボデ
ィリズモ"の中心メンバーであったS.ジョバンノ
ーニとG.ベンチュリーニのコンビ"キングコング"。
モチーフとなったのは「不思議の国のアリス」で，
客席は複雑に入り組んだいくつもの部屋からなり，
客はトリップ感覚で各部屋を行き来できるようにデ
ザインされた。部屋はそれぞれ表現方法が変えられ

ているが、素材や仕上げはシンプルで、塗装色の変化とシンボリックなパターンの変化だけで各部屋は特徴づけられている。部屋のパターンには、赤いハートのレリーフや恋人たちが交わす言葉のレタリング、恋（ハート）と死（どくろ）の組み合わせなど、メタフォリックな表現が試みられた。細長いブルーの部屋にはＴＶゲームのキャラクターを思わせる回転式スクリーンが取り付けられている。このバールは、コンピューターのアイコンや1990年代のコミックのような、新しいイメージ・コミュニケーションや共通の視覚言語を模索した空間であるとも言えよう。

MADDALENA
This fascinating bar is located in Prato, a town 20km northwest from Florence. The project was completed by designers duo King Kong of Stefano Giovannoni and Guido Venturini, leading figures of design movement Bolidismo in 1980s in Florence. The design theme of this project is a novel "Alice in Wonderland".
The interior is consisted of several rooms and guests feel like a kind of visual trip, when they come and go through each different room with simple material and finish. Varied colors and patterns of painted surfaces successfully express metaphoric symbols and icons of heart, skull, lovers letters, and so on.
In a narrow blue room, revolving screens express television game characters.
This bar will become a legendary spot in near future using new type visual expressions in this age of digital communication.

Photos by Yoichi Horimoto,
text by Masaatsu Fukazawa.

アンチ・モダニズムを表現したウイーン郊外のドライブイン・カフェ

トゥーラスト バット・フィッシャウ

オーストリア，バット・フィッシャウ

Drive-in TOURAST BAD FISCHAU

A-2721 Bad Fischau, Austria
Designer : Friedensreich Hundertwasser　Architect : Peter Pelikan

1．道路側から見た特徴ある外観ファサード。2階への階段に沿ってガラス張りの開
　　口部が設けられている
2．子供のための遊び場が設けられている裏側の庭
3．2階奥のレストラン客席からカフェ方向を見る。右側開口部の外はテラス
1．View of the facade from the road side
2．View of the courtyard for children
3．View from the restaurant area to the cafe area(2F)

1

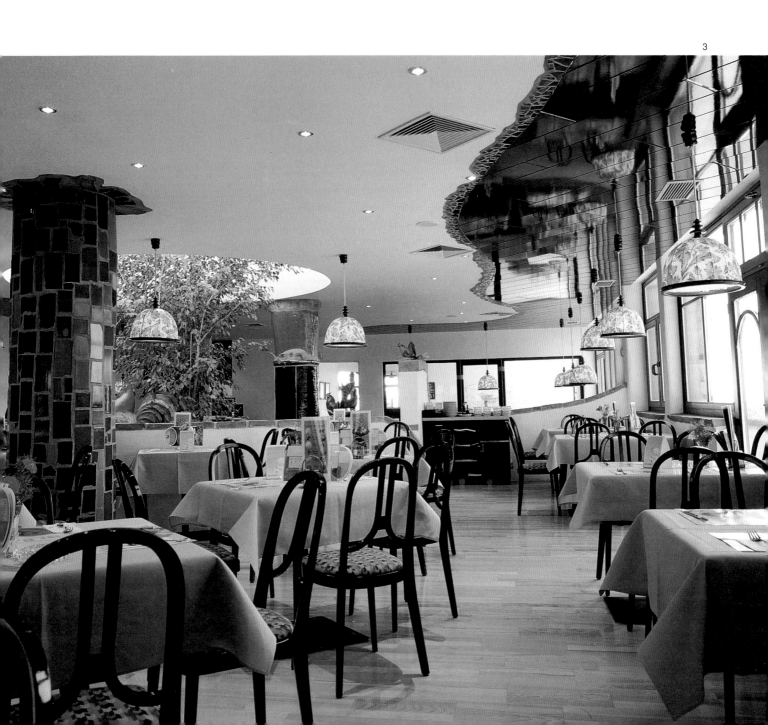

4

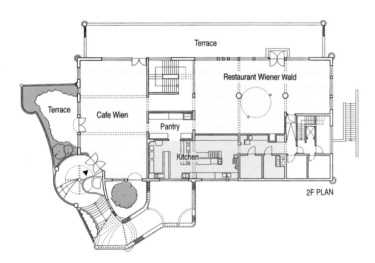

Terrace

Restaurant Wiener Wald

Terrace

Cafe Wien

Pantry

Kitchen

2F PLAN

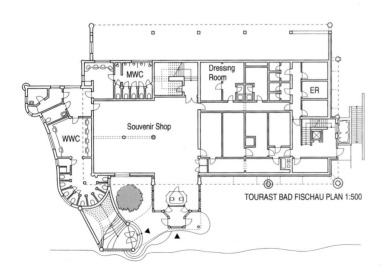

MWC

Dressing Room

ER

Souvenir Shop

WWC

TOURAST BAD FISCHAU PLAN 1:500

●画家フンデルトヴァッサーのデザイン

ウイーン生まれの画家フリーデンスライヒ・フンデルトヴァッサーのデザインによるドライブインで，ウイーンからグラーツに向かうアウトバーンを45km南下した街，バット・フィッシャウにオープンした。建物の1階は土産物店，2階は典型的なウイーン風カフェ（65席）とヨーロッパ各地にチェーンを持つファミリーレストラン「ウイーンの森」（120席）という構成になっている。140席のテラス席も設けられ，絶好の眺望を楽しむことができる。

1階にはドライブインには欠かせない，旅行者用トイレも広々と設けられた。トイレの壁面はカラフルなモザイクタイルが散りばめられ，フンデルトヴァッサーらしく床は地面に沿って微妙に波打っている。また，小さい子供連れの家族のためのおむつ交換スペースはトイレスペースから独立して設けられた。屋上には，常に自然保護の立場をとり続けるフンデルトヴァッサーの「木が育たないと思われる場所に木を植える」という思想にもとづいて土が運び込まれ，現在では見事な緑が繁っている。この建物は，もともとは50年代に建てられた，特長のない殺伐としたRC建築をリニューアルしたものである。改築にはフンデルトヴァッサー専属の建築家，P.ペリカンが協力している。

TOURAST BAD FISCHAU

Viennese painter Friedensreich Hundertwasser designed this drive-in in Bad Fischau, a town 45km south from Autobahn going from Vienna to Graz. The first floor is a souvenir shop and the second floor is Weinerwald, a typical chained roadside cafe and restaurant in Europe. 140 seats are available on a terrace, where guests enjoy a fine view.

The restroom, a must-space in drive-ins, is spacious and decorated by colorful mosaic tiles on the walls and floor level is uneven, which shows characteristic Humdertwasser style. There is also a room for diapers change beside washrooms. Plants grow high on the rooftop, as the designer expresses his thoughts that he would plant wherever he decide, even if it seems to be impossible at first sight. Thus a 1950s prosaic reinforced concrete building was renovated as an intriguing project cooperated by Peter Pelikan, an architect under contract to Hundertwasser.

Photos by Henning Queren,
text by Hanae Komachi

4．1階の土産物売り場奥にある女性用トイレ。フンデルトヴァッサーらしいオーガニックなデザイン
5．タイル貼りの樹がスカイライトを支える2階入り口ホールまわり
4．Interior view of the women's toilet(1F)
5．View of the ceramic tree from the staircase (2F)

ロッテルダムのパノラミック・リバーサイド・カフェ

ボーンピェス

オランダ, ロッテルダム

Cafe Restaurant BOOMPJES

Boompjes 701, 3011XZ Rotterdam, The Netherlands
Designer : MECANOO Chris de Weijer, Erik Van Egeraat and Francine Houben

１．道路側に張り出した中３階のレストラン客席をマース川北岸に沿った遊歩道から見る
２．巨大なオブジェに囲まれたテラス席を前面に持つ西面外観。２階フロアと遊歩道がほぼ同じレベル
１．View of the north facade from the promenade
２．View of the art object and west facade

1

●ガラス張りのシャープな外観

オランダ第2の都市ロッテルダムは、ライン川と
その2本の支流マース川、スヘルト川が北海に注
ぐデルタ地帯に発達した港町である。このレスト
ランは、市街地から少し離れたマース川北岸の、
遊歩道の一角に建てられた。建物は三方がガラス
張りの開放的な造りになっており、エッジの利い
たシャープな外観を持つ。

回転式のドアを入るとバーとカフェコーナーがあ
り、その奥がレストランスペースとなっている。
川側の開口部は水面に迫り出すように傾斜してお
り、客席に着くと、ダイナミックな眺望と相まっ
て、レストランごと水に浮かんでいるような錯覚
を覚える。また、客席には中2階が設けられ、ど
の席からもマース川の景観を楽しむことができる
よう設計された。ウエーブを描くルーフラインは
空間にも動きを与えており、50年代のデザインを
模した照明器具がインテリアのアクセントとなっ
ている。屋外には大きなテラスがあり、日光浴が
好きなオランダ人の人気を得ている。

BOOMPJES

Rotterdam, the second largest city in the
Netherlands, has been developed as a pivotal
port in a delta where the Rhine and the
tributary rivers crossed and poured into the
North Sea.
This cafe and restaurant is situated on a
corner of a promenade along the north bank
of the Maas. It is open and carefree with
shapely edged exterior, and three sides of the
building is widely glazed. Entering a revolving
door, you will see a bar and cafe, and a
restaurant in the back. River side openings
are projected slantwise over the river, so you
feel like the restaurant is floating on the river,
helped with a panoramic view. Mezzanine
also lets customers enjoy seeing different
views of the Maas River. Wavy roof line
makes rhythm in the architectural space. A
fifty's style lighting accentuates the interior.
Outdoor nice terrace is popular for local
customers, for people in this county like to
take a sunbath.

Photos and text by Yoichi Horimoto

3. 中3階客席からパノラミックに広がる窓外の
   景色を見る。2階の半分を中3階にしたこと
   で、どの客席からも外部の景色を楽しむこと
   ができる
3 Panoramic view of the river from the
   dining area(M3F)

3

4．中3階客席から遊歩道側に張り出した客席コーナー方向を見る
View from the restaurant area to the promenade(M3F)

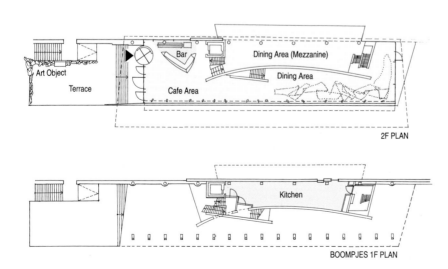

Art Object

Terrace

Bar

Cafe Area

Dining Area (Mezzanine)

Dining Area

2F PLAN

Kitchen

BOOMPJES 1F PLAN

ロランジェ・ブルー

ベルギー，ブリュッセル

Cafe L'ORANGE BLEU

29 Rue A.Dansert, 1000 Brussel, Belgium
Designer : Raoul Cavadias

1．奥の客席Bから入り口側客席A方向を見る　View from the room B to the room A

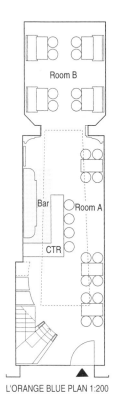

L'ORANGE BLUE PLAN 1:200

3

●オレンジ色の空間と緑色の骨董家具
ヨーロッパの政治拠点となりつつあるブリュッセルの、証券取引所以西のダウンタウン地区にできたカフェで、元ヘアサロンだった空間を改装し、オープンした。
店内はオレンジ色を基調として空間全体のカラートーンが整えられており、オーナーが所蔵する18世紀の骨董カウンターや家具は修復され、濃緑色に着色されて店の中央に据えられている。このほか、店内で使用しているテーブル、イスなどもオーナーのコレクションを修復したものである。正面奥の部屋はヘアサロン当時の意匠がそのまま流用された。行灯照明が仕組まれた天井や壁には、17世紀のイタリア絨毯のバロック・パターンをコピーした厚手のトレーシングペーパーが張り巡らされ、クラシックなガラス器のような透明感を生み出している。天井には天幕が架けられ、設計者自身の手による金属の造作と相まって全体的にはネオ・バロック風の空間にまとめられた。このカフェは、古い建

物の中に新しいスノッブな店が出来つつある一角に位置しており、夜は深夜2時まで営業し、来店者も午後10時過ぎにピークを迎える。

L'ORANGE BLEU
This cafe, renovated from a hair salon, opened in the west area from the city of stockbrokers area in downtown Brussels, representing the character of this future-central city of the EU.
Orange color strikes the keynote of the interior color scheme. The 18th century counter and antique furniture of the owner's collection are restored, painted dark green, and displayed around the center. Tables and chairs are also from his collection. The original decoration for the hair salon is used for the back space. The ceiling and walls with built-in lamps covered with thick tracing paper of the of 17th century

Italian Baroque rug pattern. It shows transparence of a kind of classical glass. Tents are suspending from the ceiling.
With a designer's hand made metal work, the interior has an atmosphere of Neo-Baroque style.
As the neighborhood is full of hip shops and cafes, this cafe is mostly crowded after ten and the closing time is 2 am.

Photos and text by Yoichi Horimoto

2．奥客席Bのトレーシングペーパーを効果的に使った光り壁と光り天井。表面に古いイタリア絨毯のパターンをコピーして使用
3．地下への階段途中から見た客席A
2．View of the lighting wall and ceiling in the room B
3．View from the stairs to the room A

芸術歴史博物館のカフェハウス

ウイーンの歴史を物語る大ホールに設けられたカフェハウス

オーストリア，ウイーン

KAFFEEHAUS DES KUNSTHISTORISCHEN MUSEUMS

Maria-Theresien Platz, Wien, Austria
Designer : Gert M.Mayr-Keber

1．博物館1階から2階カフェハウスへ通じる中央階段ホールの天井画
2．ホール客席を3階フロアレベルのギャラリーから見る。空間は既存のままで照明器具のみが新設された
1．View of the center stairwell to the cafe house
2．View of the hall area from the gallery

1

2

3

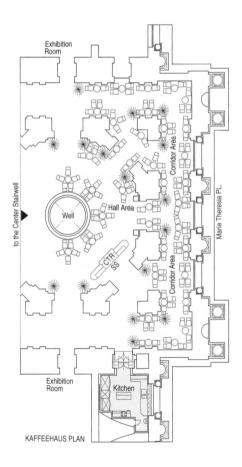

Exhibition Room

Corridor Area

to the Center Stairwell

Well

Hall Area

CTR SS

Corridor Area

Maria Theresia PL.

Exhibition Room

Kitchen

KAFFEEHAUS PLAN

●100年を隔てた二つの世紀末の意匠

イタリア・ルネッサンス様式の芸術歴史博物館は、皇帝フランツ・ヨゼフの下、1872年から1891年にかけて建設された歴史的建造物である。建物はウィーンのマリア・テレジア広場に面し、中2階37室、2階40室の展示室を持ち、ヨーロッパ絵画のコレクションは世界有数を誇る。この建物の2階の円蓋吹き抜け大ホールに、休憩と軽食のためのカフェハウスが新設された。このカフェのデザインにおいて、設計者のグラーツ工科大学出身のG.マイル・ケーバーは、19世紀と20世紀、二つの世紀末の意匠とマテリアルの相互干渉を最小限に抑え、両者をみごとに調和させた。フロアに置かれたグラマラスな休息イスのカバーには、往時からの白黒大理石によるフロアパターンが、コンピュータでアレンジされて転写されている。濃厚なディテールに満たされた吹き抜け大空間の中空には、細パイプで支持される円盤状の照明器具が軽やかに浮かび、また、各種設備やケーブル、配水管などは設備パイプに統合され、吹き抜け中空に巡らされている。フロアパターンはイスのカバー同様にデザイン加工され、カフェで使われる陶磁器の模様にもなっている。

KAFFEEHAUS DES KUNSTHISTORIS-CHEN MUSEUMS

The Museum of Art History by Italian Renaissance style was built from 1872 to 1891 by Franz Josef I. in front of Maria-Theresien Platz. The exhibition area is consisted of 37 rooms on the mezzanine floor and 40 ones on the second level. The collection of European painting of this museum is one of the world's most prominent ones. A cafe was created in a dome hall on the second floor.

G.M. Mayr-Keber, a designer of this project who studied at Graz Technical University, combines two fin-de-ciecle styles of the 19th and 20th century, keeping harmony of different elements and materials. Using computer graphic, classical black and white checker floor pattern is redesigned and printed on glamourous covers of chairs.The pattern is also used for porcelains.

In midair of the dome decorated densely, a disk-shaped light is supported by fine pipes. Various utilities pipes and ducts are bundled and go across the space.

Photos by Henning Queren,
text by Hanae Komachi

3．円形吹き抜けの手すり周囲に配された客席
4．ホール周囲の回廊部分を利用した客席。外側はマリア・テレジア広場
3．View of the hall area surrounding well
4．View of the corridor area to the kitchen side

1910年代の廃倉庫を改装したベルギー・ゲント市のカフェ・レストラン

パックハウス

ベルギー，ゲント

Restaurant Tearoom PAKHUIS

Schuurkenstraat 4, 9000 Gent, Belgium
Designer : Antonio Pinto

1

●元倉庫の構造を生かす
東フランダース州の州都，ゲント市中心街のコーレイ広場に通じる裏通りにこのカフェ・レストランはある。"パックハウス"の店名が示すように，建物自体は1910年代に建設された元倉庫で，長年使われることなく放置されていた。この店は元倉庫の基本的な構造を残し，全面的に改装して飲食店へと再生させたものである。
店内はこの建物の構造体である鋳物の柱を空間分割のエレメントとして使い，倉庫としての大空間のビスタを残しながら，1階と中2階の空間全体をレストラン，バー，ティールームの三つの業態・機能に区分している。また，北ヨーロッパの暗く長い冬を明るく快適に過ごせるよう，自然光を積極的に採り入れるため，レストラン部分の天井は天窓化された。色彩計画は，構造の金属部分をパステルグリーンに着色し，カウンターなどの木部はパステルブラウンにカラーリングされ，ナチュラル志向の落ち着いた環境をつくり出すことに成功している。

PAKHUIS
This cafe and restaurant is in a back streets to the central place in Gent, the capital of East Flanders state. As the name indicates, the original site was a warehouse built in 1910s left for a long time idly. The sweeping renovation transformed it into this bar and restaurant.
Using casted construction columns to separate space, the interior keeps a wide view and is functionally divided into three areas : a restaurant, a bar, and a tearoom for the first floor and the mezzanine.
The ceiling is glazed to get sun light as much as possible for customers to feel comfortable during long cold winter. Construction metal parts are painted pastel green and wood parts like a counter are pastel brown, which creates natural feeling in the interior.

Photos and text by Yoichi Horimoto

1．1階入り口左側のレジ前からティールームへ抜ける階段方向を見る
2．1階左側半分を占めるティールームと円形バーカウンターを2階から見る
1．View from the cashier side to the tearoom(1F)
2．View of the tearoom area and bar counter from the second floor

100

4

3．2階客席から見た吹き抜けまわり全景。鋳鉄の構造柱をそのまま使うことにより倉庫
　のイメージを色濃く残している
4．1階右側のレストラン客席から2階へのアプローチ階段まわりを見る
3．View from the second floor to the center well
4．View of the stairs from the dining area(1F)

5

5．隣棟との連絡通路であったブリッジを改装した個室客席
6．入り口まわり外観。左側上部にブリッジを改装した個室客席が見える
5．Interior view of the restaurant room(2F)
6．View of the Facade and entry

6

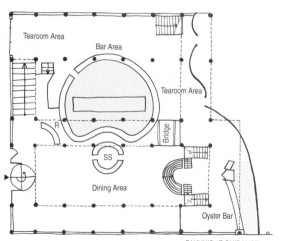

PAKHUIS 1F GUIDANCE

2本の木橋が交差する台北のイタリアンファストフード

ジャストエム

台湾，台北

Restaurant JUST 'M'

Chung Hsaio E.RD. SEC IV, Taipei, Taiwan
Designer : P.T.C.O. Architects & Designers, Mark Lintott and David Connor

1．店内奥の3層に吹き抜けた空間を地下1階から上へ見る　View of the high well and bridge from the basement floor

2

●マニファクチュアの金物ディテール

台北市にできた3層のイタリア料理店で，イギリス人の建築家が設計を手掛けた。店内は地下1階と1階がファストフード的なスピード重視のダイニングで，2階はフルサービスの本格的なイタリア料理店になっている。建物は細長く短辺の一方に入り口があり，店内の奥方向へいかに客を導入するかがデザインのポイントとなった。デザイン上の特長として挙げられるのは店内奥の2本のブリッジである。設計者は，閉塞感のある細長い空間にダイナミックな空間的魅力を創出するため，フロア奥に地下1階から2階までの3層の吹き抜けを設け，その吹き抜け1，2階部分にそれぞれブリッジを渡した。客はこの橋を渡って自然に奥へと導入されるよう計画されている。木製の橋は金属のジョイントで支持され，そのディテールが空間のアクセントにもなっている。また，壁面は手工業的な金属のコーナージョイントで固定された木製パネルが使われ，レンガ粉混入のプラスター壁とともに，近代建築黎明期のヨーロッパ建築の雰囲気を感じさせる空間となった。

JUST 'M'

A British architect designed a three floor level Italian restaurant in Taipei, Taiwan. The first floor and basement floor are like a fast food dining area, the second floor an authentic restaurant. The building is oblong and narrow, so the point was how to bring in customers from the entrance of small facade to inner part of the restaurant. To create a sense of dynamism in the interior, the designer constructs an open ceiling space from the basement up to the second floor and he erected two bridges across the void of first and second floor. Two bridges are powerful and they efficiently and smoothly lead customers. The bridges are wooden and supported by metal joints whose decorative details themselves appeal to us. Wooden panel with metal corner joints are used for walls, together with plaster walls mixed with brick powder, produce an atmospher of European architecture at the dawn of Modern age.

Photos by Nick Wang,
text by Mark Lintott

2．地下1階のファストフード・エリアから見た階段まわりとブリッジ
3．同じく地下1階のファストフード・エリア壁面ディテール

2．View of the stairs and bridge in the fast food area(B1F)

3．Details of the wall(B1F)

3

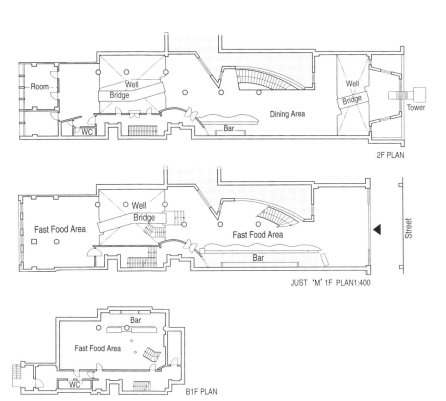

2F PLAN

JUST 'M' 1F PLAN1:400

B1F PLAN

廃線となったミラノ郊外の市電駅舎をバールに再生

アティエンメ

イタリア，ミラノ

Bar ATIEMME

Bastioni di Porta Volta, 15 Milano, Italy
Designer : Rosauba Angeloni, Antonio Quaranta

1

1．路面電車の始発駅をそのまま残した外観
2．左奥の客席Aから中央カウンター方向を見る
3．マジョルカ陶器を貼り合わせた中央カウンターから客席Aを見る
1．View of the existing facade from the street
2．Full view of the interior from the seatings A
3．View from the counter to the seatings A

2

4．カウンターわきの柱を利用した客席Ａの円形待合席
View of the waiting bench between the counter and seatings A

●市電の駅からコミュニケーション・ステーションへ
ムッソリーニのファシズム政権の終焉と戦後の混
乱期を経て、ミラノでは急速に進む都市化と人口
増加が問題となり、その対策として郊外都市計画
が立てられた。1950年代後半のことである。この
計画と並行して都市と郊外を結ぶ路面電車網が拡
大するが、1970年代に入り、路面電車が徐々に姿
を消し始め、廃線の駅舎は都市交通営団の事務所
として使われ、やがて、廃駅舎は一般にも貸し出
されるようになった。このバールも1950年代に建
設された路面電車の始発駅舎の一つを転用したも
のである。バールには都市交通営団の略称「ＡＴ
Ｍ」を音読みした「アティエンメ」が店名として
付けられた。このプロジェクトには、いわゆるデ
ザイナーは参画せず、バールの企画・経営者であ
る女性のスケッチを職人が具現化する共同作業で
店づくりが進められた。イスは払い下げで1950年
代のカステリ製、は虫類のようなバーカウンター
のエッジは手打ちの鉛板で、バーの腰壁はマジョ
ルカ陶器を貼り合わせたものである。駅舎はイン
パクトのある色彩と造形が与えられ、人々のコミ
ュニティの駅として再生した。

ATIEMME
After the end of Mussolini's Fascism
government and the successive post-war
chaotic period, Milan came to suffer rapid
urbanization and population explosion, and
the city planned urban development projects
in the late 1950s. With the urbanization, tram
network expanded as an essential transportation system. In 1970s, tram cars gradually
disappeared and the station buildings of
abandoned lines came to be used as offices
of municipal transit authority, and so on.
This bar is renovated from such an abandoned 1950s station building. The name
ATIEMME is an abbreviation of the transit
authority. Upon sketches by a planner and
owner, this project was completed by
collaboration work of builders, and no
professional designers participated in it.
Chairs are disposed items of 1950s Castelli
made. A reptilian shaped bar counter edge is
hand made lead, and counter tops and sides
are covered with Majorca tiles. Thanks to
striking colors and elements, this old building
came back to life as a communication station.

Photos by Yoichi Horimoto,
text by Fumihiko Hirayama

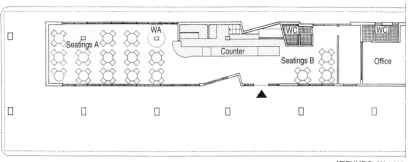

ATIEMME PLAN 1:300

リニューアルされたパリ歓楽街の老舗カフェ

ピガール
フランス，パリ

Cafe PIGALLE
22 Blvd. de Clichy, 75018 Paris, France
Designer : Pierangelo Caramia

1．入り口右側テラス席からカウンター席と2階への階段まわりを見る　View of the counter and stairs from the terrace area(1F)

2

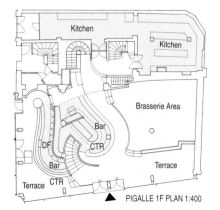

▲ PIGALLE 1F PLAN 1:400

Kitchen
Kitchen
Brasserie Area
Bar
DF
CTR
Bar
CTR
Terrace
Terrace

2F PLAN

Office
MWC
WWC
Dining A
Dining B

●若者のナイトカルチュアの拠点

ピガール界隈は、老舗キャバレー"ムーラン・ルージュ"の風車のサインに代表される、パリの古くからの歓楽街として知られてきた。現在ではセックスショップや観光客相手のディスコやクラブ、ヌードシアターが通りに軒を連ね、色街的な空気が残る一帯である。しかし、モラリストが顔をしかめるこの界隈も、流行に敏感な遊び好きの20代やゲイ・カルチュアの担い手たちにより、若者のナイトカルチュアの重要な地域となりつつある。パリの夜のショービジネスの拠点であった時代から、この通りに店を構えていた"カフェ・ピガール"は改装され、新しいナイトシーンの舞台として生まれ変わった。フロアは2層になっており、1階にはバーとテラス形式のブラッセリー、2階はダイニングホールとなっている。客席には設計者のオリジナルデザインによる"ピガール・チェア"が置かれ、その後、このイスは家具メーカーによる商品化もなされている。デザイナーのP.カラミアは、80年代、イタリア・フィレンツェを中心に起きたデザイン・ムーブメント"ボリディズモ"の中心メンバーの一人でもある。

PIGALLE

Pigalle, an old famous district of pleasure symbolized by Moulin Rouge, is now a kind of tourists red light zone full of sex shops, discos, and striptease theaters. Although old conservative generation frowns at this area, it is getting more popular, as one of centers of subculture and night life in Paris, particularly for fashionable 20s and gay people.
Cafe Pigalle has been open when this area was a mecca of show business, and it has renovated as a new stage for night scene. The first floor is a bar and brasserie with a terrace and the second floor is a dining room. On the first floor, custom-made Pigalle chairs are used, which are now commercialized. Pierangelo Caramia, a designer of the cafe, was one of leading figures of a design movement Bolidismo started in 80s Florence.

Photos by Anders Edström,
text by Takeji Hirakawa

3

4

2．1階右奥を占めるブラッセリーの壁側客席
3．1階入り口部より階段を通して右奥のブラッセリー客席方向を見る
4．2階の階段吹き抜け手すりから下部の1階カウンター席を見る
2．View of the brasserie area from the bar side(1F)
3．View from the entry to the brasserie area
4．View from the second floor to the counter through the stairwell

海をイメージしたトロントの巨大ビリヤーズ・バー＆クラブ

シャークシティ・アスレチッククラブ

カナダ，トロント

SHARK CITY ATHLETIC CLUB

117 Eglinton Ave.East, Toronto, Ontario, Canada
Designer : II BY IV

1．1階入り口側の待合スペースからダイニング客席とバーカウンターを仕切る異形鉄筋
　のスクリーンを見る
2．階段の踊り場から見た1階と地下1階の店内。左側に1階の待合スペース、右上にバ
　ーカウンターが見える
1．View of the steel rods screen dividing dining area and bar(1F)
2．View from the landing to the first floor and basement floor

3

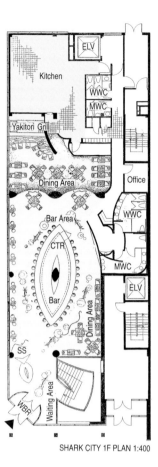

SHARK CITY 1F PLAN 1:400

4

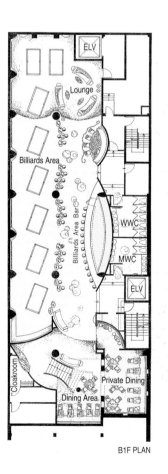

B1F PLAN

5

●海を直喩する造形と色彩
この店にはアスレチッククラブという名前が付い
ているが，フィットネスクラブではない。地下に
は8台のビリヤード台が置かれ，総床面積は
1115m²という2層の大型ナイトクラブである。客
はお酒や食事，音楽，ビリヤードを楽しみながら，
この広いフロアを自由に動き回ることができる。
1階はボートをかたどったバーカウンターが中央
に置かれ，床面には温かみのある色彩が使われて
おり，日没時の海をイメージさせるデザインでま
とめられた。バーカウンターにはムラノガラスの
断片を混ぜて研ぎだしたテラゾが使われている。
一方，ラセン階段で下りると，地下フロアはやや
暗く，海底を思わせる色調で統一されている。海
草のような金属の造形や水泡のドアノブ，窓の中
の喫水線など，各種ディテールにも海底をモチー
フとする造形が演出的に用いられた。地下のバー
は壁に沿って11mも長く延び，バートップの素材
にはブラジル産の青い花崗岩が採用されている。

インテリアのイメージとなったのは "穏やかでキ
ラキラ輝いた海" で，このイメージが，日没の穏
やかな水面と "シャークシティ" という海底の遊
技場に展開された。

SHARK CITY ATHLETIC CLUB
Of course this is not a fitness club, although
its name uses a words athletic club. This is a
two floor level big night club on the total floor
area of 1,115 square meters. The basement
level is a pool bar with eight billiard tables.
Enjoying alcohol, meal, music, billiards,
customers swim in the air of pleasure
aquarium. The first floor is designed by a
theme of sunset scene of the sea. A boat-
shaped counter is in the center and the floor
uses warm colors. The counter is decorated
terrazzo mixed with crushed Murano glass.
Going down a spiral stairs, you will arrive the
basement level designed upon colors and
images of the seabed : metal work seaweed,

bubble detail door nobs, the water lines of
windows. The basement bar counter runs 11
meters, and the counter top is made of
Brazilian blue granite. The calm and shinning
sea is the core design concept. Shark city
represents it two ways.

Photos by David Whitaker,
text by Masaaki Takahashi

3．地下1階の左側半分を占めるビリヤード・エリ
　アをバーサイドから見る
4．地下1階の最奥コーナーにあるラウンジエリア
5．地下1階のビリヤード・エリアとバーの間に配
　されたドリンクテーブルから奥のラウンジ方向
　を見る
3．View of the billiards area from the bar area
　(B1F)
4．View of the lounge area from the billiards
　area(B1F)
5．View from the billiards area to the lounge
　area(B1F)

リスボンのナイトシーンをリードするカフェ&ビリヤーズクラブ

アルカンターラ・カフェ

ポルトガル，リスボン

Restaurant Bar ALCANTARA CAFE

Rua Maria Lufsa Holstein 15, 1300 Lisboa, Portugal
Designer : Antonio Pinto

1．入り口側から待合スペースを通してビリヤード・コーナーを見る。左側に置かれた人形がアイキャッチ
の役割を果たしている
2．バーカウンター前の通路から見た待合スペース。突き当たり右側が入り口、左側がビリヤードコーナー
1．View of the waiting area from the entry to the billiards area
2．View from the bar area to the waiting area

3

●リスボンのユースカルチュア・センター
このクラブはリスボンの街の中心街から少し離れたアルカンターラ地区の静かな石畳の舗道沿いにある。店舗は元倉庫だった建物を改装したものである。周囲には数店のディスコを始めとした若者向けのナイトスポットが多い。この店もオープン直後からこの地区の若者文化の中心的な存在となり、このクラブに出掛けることが一つの流行にまでなった。
店内はエントランスから入って、まずバーコーナーがあり、その奥がビリヤード・ルームになっている。さらに奥に進むと大きなロフト空間のサンルームになっており、右側がレストラン、左側にはカフェが配されている。インテリアは「鉄の時代」の橋梁を思わせる、量感のある鉄の柱梁と鋲打ちの鉄板で力強く構築されており、それらはブロンズ古色仕上げでまとめられた。この空間の中には、サモトラケのニケ像を始めとする巨大なギリシャ彫刻像のレプリカが数点据えられている。このクラブは別棟にアートギャラリーも持っていて、文化的なアート活動を側面から支援している。

3．店内奥側レストラン客席の光り壁を中央より
　　見る
4．店内奥側レストラン客席のミラー貼り壁面と
　　リベット打ちの鉄製柱形に取り付けられたブ
　　ロンズ古色仕上げのブラケット照明
3．View of the dining area to the lighting wall
4．View of the mirror wall and lighting fixture
　　in the dining area

ALCANTARA CAFE
Alcantara is a name of a suburb area little bit far from the center of Lisboa city. This club is situated in there on a quiet stone pavement road. The neighborhood has many clubs, discos, and other spots for the young. This project was a renovation of a warehouse. Soon after the opening, this bar attracted many young men and women and made itself a vogues in Lisbon night life.
There are a bar near the entrance, and the next area is a billiard room. In the far back, sunroom with a restaurant on the right and a cafe on the left. In the interior, heavy-and-strong-looking columns and beams covered by iron plates with rivets are reminiscence of a bridge built in the age of steel. Their finishes are fake rusted bronze. Moreover, a number of Greek classical sculptures like Nike of Samotráki are displayed. The annex building is a gallery to patronize cultural events.

Photos by Yoichi Horimoto,
text by Masaatsu Fukazawa

バルセロナ・スタイルのバールの伝統を守るグラフィック幻惑空間

セルツ

スペイン，バルセロナ

Bar SELTS-Aperitifs and Tapas

Rossello154, Barcelona, Spain
Designer : Dani Freixes, Victor Arganti, Vicente Miranda

1．店内中央トイレ前の階段から奥の客席を見る。床と壁面が発光するグラフィック面
　　で構成された特徴ある空間
2．店内奥の客席通路からカウンター席を通して入り口方向を見る。壁面のグラフィッ
　　クは食前酒のロゴをモチーフにしている
1．View of the lighting floor and wall from the stairs
2．View of the counter area to the entry side

2

1

●食前酒のロゴに包まれて酒を飲む
スペインのバールの特徴でもあった"食前酒とタ
パス（惣菜料理）"の伝統は，新しいバールでは
忘れ去られる傾向にある。このバールの伝統を再
認識させる場として過激に登場したのがこの店で
ある。内照式のガラス壁面には代表的な食前酒の
よく知られた巨大なロゴマークが並び，バックバ
ーの壁面にはチョークで本日のタパス・メニュー
が手書きで書き出される。このカンパリやマルテ
ィニなどの食前酒のロゴは，スペインの伝統的な
バールのスタイルを人々に連想させるもので，こ
の店のコンセプトの象徴でもある。これらを強調

する圧倒的な環境グラフィックは床面から壁面に
まで展開され、この店の印象を決定づける重要な
ファクターとなった。壁面の素材は基本的に発光
するガラスと黒板用の青い壁だけといっていい。
空間は間口が約4〜6m、奥行きが33mというと
ても細長い空間で、約23mの直線カウンターが全
体の空間を貫いている。さらに奥の間口が広めの
空間は地上レベルより1m上げられた中2階と半
地下に分けられた。これによって店内は、入り口
側のバーと奥のサロン的なスペースに区分され、
"大人数を受け入れる快適なバール"という経営
サイドの要求も満たしたものとなっている。

SELTS

Spanish bars' tradition "aperitifs and tapas" is
gradually getting neglected in new type bars. To
revive this good dining custom, Selts opened
drastically. Big logos of famous aperitifs brands
are decorated on the glass wall with built-in
lighting. Tapas menu are written by hand with a
chalk on the blackboard behind a counter.
These logos of Campali, Martini, etc are a kind
of reminder of old type bar for Spanish people
and it is the representative element of this bar.
The big graphic decorations are displayed on
the floor level and on the wall, so they look very
impressive. Wall materials are just glass with
built-in lamps and blue board for writing
board.

The site is narrow : the frontage is from four to
six meter, the depth is 33 meters. 24 meters
straight counter goes across the interior. Back
area with wider space is divided into two : a one
meter raised floor area and a half basement
level area. The varied floor level makes open
bar near the entrance and a salon-like bar in the
back. It fulfills the owner's requirements to
accept a large number of people.

Photos by Terresa Miró, text by Masayo Ave

3．店内奥のトイレ前から見たソファ席　View of the sofa seatings from the toilet side

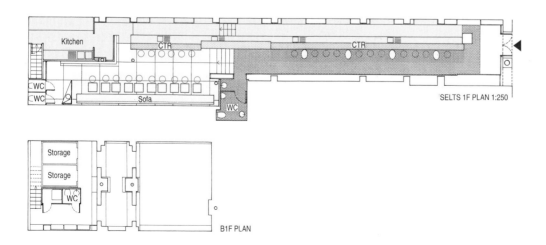

SELTS 1F PLAN 1:250

B1F PLAN

BARS & DISCOS

世界のバー＆ディスコ

中世のタワーゲートを変身させたバルセロナのバー

トーレ・デ・アビラ

スペイン、バルセロナ

Bar TORES DE AVILA

Spanish Village, Barcelona, Spain
Designer : Alfredo Arribas and Javier Mariscal

１．向かって左側 "ムーンタワー" 屋上の "月" をシンボライズしたオブジェから右側 "サンタワー" 方向を見る
２．"サンタワー" ３階ラウンジエリア客席をエレベーター側から吹き抜け方向へ見る
１．Night view of the roof terrace from the moon tower side
２．View of the lounge from the elevator side in the sun tower(3F)

1

3

4

●劇場のようなバーティカル空間

バルセロナの民族村・スパニッシュビレッジに移築されていた，二つのタワーを持つ既存の中世の門をバー空間に改造したプロジェクト。観光客の多い立地条件から，ゲート両脇の1階はすべてトイレとされ，外部から直接2階へアプローチするブリッジ階段を設けることから計画はスタートした。二つのタワーの外観と大きさは同じであるが，内部空間は対照的なデザインコンセプトでまとめられている。

向かって左側のムーン・タワーは，女性，夜，月，曲線などをテーマとし，2階のバーフロアから3層分の高さを持つ吹き抜けの空間には，光ファイバーを張りめぐらした"夜空の皮膜"が配され，回転することにより舞台裏の仕組みまで見せる。右側サン・タワーのテーマは，男性，昼，太陽，直線などで，左側と同じ高さを持つ吹き抜け空間には，中央に円形の穴があいた"四角い天空"が吊り下げられている。

この二つの空間に共通するのは，連続する垂直空間によって視線が変化していくことで，劇場空間のように人々は場所を変えながら，俳優になったり，観客になったりすることができるのである。

TORES DE AVILA

A Middle Ages gate with two towers was moved to the Spanish Village as a part of the cultural amusement center. This bar is a renovation project of the gate. As the Spanish Village is one of famous sightseeing spots, the first floor of the both sides of the gate has rest rooms and a bridge connecting directly from the first to the second floor. It was the first step of designing this project. The two towers are seemingly almost same in their size and shape, but the interior is contrastingly different each other.

The tower on the left side you face is designed by motifs of women, night, moon, and curve lines, and from bar on the second floor, you see in a three floor level open ceiling "skin of night sky" decorated with optical fiber. It goes round like a revolving stage. The tower on the right uses themes of men, day, sun, and straight lines. It has also the same open ceiling with "square sky" decorative element is hanging and the square has a round hall in the center. Vertical space planning catches our attention dramatically and it makes us like an audience of a theater, when we move in the interior.

Photos by Jordi Sarra

3．右側"サンタワー"の上階レベルから見た3階ラウンジ吹き抜けまわり客席
4．左側"ムーンタワー"2階入り口側上部の階段吹き抜けを飾る布のオブジェ
5．同じく"ムーンタワー"2階のバーエリア客席と上部吹き抜けに張り出したデッキ席。デッキ席の上部には光ファイバーによる星空のスクリーンが設けられている
3．View of the lounge and well in the sun tower(3F)
4．View of the stairwell and textile art object in the moon tower(2F)
5．View of the bar area and deck seatings in the moon tower(2F)

6

7

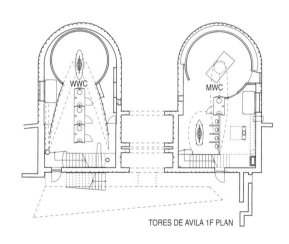

3F PLAN

2F PLAN

TORES DE AVILA 1F PLAN

6．"ムーンタワー"の光ファイバースクリーンはデッキごと回転し，配線など
　背後の舞台裏まで見せる
7．"ムーンタワー"1階の広々とした女性用トイレ。中央にメーキャップ用テ
　ーブル，周辺には休憩用のソファが配されている
6．Back side view of the opticl fiber screen in the moon tower(3F)
7．View of the women's powder room in the moon tower(1F)

ロンドンの地下洞穴を彩るＳＦ的な世界

ジョーンズ・バー＆レストラン

イギリス，ロンドン

JONES Bar & Restaurant

35 Earlham Street, Covent Garden, London WC2H, England
Designer : Quentin Reynold

１．客席Ａから見た入り口扉まわり。外側にエントランスホールと受付がある　View of the entrance door from the dining A side

2

3

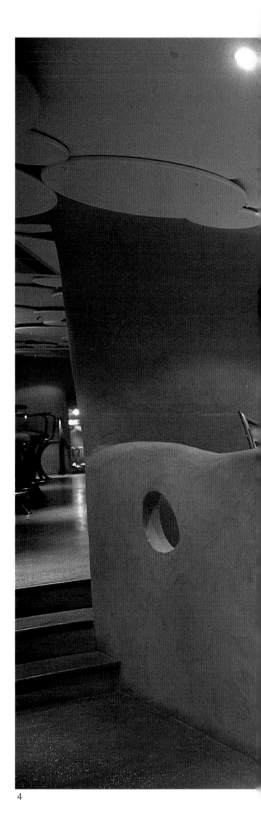

4

2．店内奥のバーコーナーからカウンター席を通して入り口方向を見る
3．カウンター席に面した待合スペースのソファ
4．入り口から右側の客席Ａを見る。天井にはＭＤＦボードの円盤が雲
　のように浮かんでいる
2．View from the bar area to the entry side
3．View of the waiting area from the bar counter
4．View of the dining A from the entry

●ローコストを克服した隠れ家的な飲食空間
ロンドンでも個性的な若者の集まる街，コベント・
ガーデンのアールハム・ストリート。この通りにで
きた話題のビアレストラン"ベルゴ・セントラール"
の斜め前にあるショッピングビルの地下に，時期を
同じくしてこのレストラン＆バーはオープンした。
プロジェクトはローコストの上，途中でそれまでデ
ザインを担当していた設計者がクライアントと衝突
し，続行が危ぶまれていたのを，ピンチヒッター的
に引き受けるという悪条件であった。まったくの準
備期間なしでスタートした現場工事が，なんとか
完成にこぎ着けたのは，引き受けた職人たちの技量

によるものといえよう。
デザインのコンセプトは、地下の納骨堂、または
洞穴のようなスペースであり、自然光の入らないと
いう条件を逆に強調するという手法が取られた。エ
クスパンドメタル・シートの下地に砂壁塗装を施
した曲面の壁と天井を持つアプローチ空間を通って、
地下の店内に入ると、そこには様々なSFの映画、
コミックス、小説の世界を集積し、折衷した独特
の世界が広がる。火星人の侵略戦争に抵抗した人
間たちが地下空間に集まるH.G.ウエルズのSF小
説のように、人々は地下のSF空間に身を隠し、非
日常的な世界を楽しむのである。

JONES BAR & RESTAURANT

On Earlham Street, a fashionable area near
Covent Garden, London, Jones Bar &
Restaurant is located just on the opposite side
of Belgo Centraal, a newly opened trendy
beer restaurant. The project is in the basement level.

The clash between an original designer and
the client nearly broke down the project, and a
new designer filled in and completed it. It was
partly due to skills and techniques of builders
that the project was accomplished somehow.
The design concept is a catacomb, a cave, or

something like that. Interesting thing is that
this project exaggerates blocking the natural
light.

The curved walls and the ceiling of an
approach are covered with rough sand coat
on expanded metal sheets. It takes you to the
wonderland full of images of sci-fi movies,
comics, novels, etc. People enjoy this basement shelter like one in a novel by H.G.Wells,
where people take refuge from the attack of
Martians.

Photos by Henning Queren,
text by Hanae Komachi

5

6

5．入り口左側に配された客席Ｂのアルコーブ風ボックス席
6．店内最奥の客席Ｃ。壁のアルミ製照明器具は初期のＳＦ映画からイメージされた
5．View of the alcove room in the dining B
6．View of the seatings in the dining C

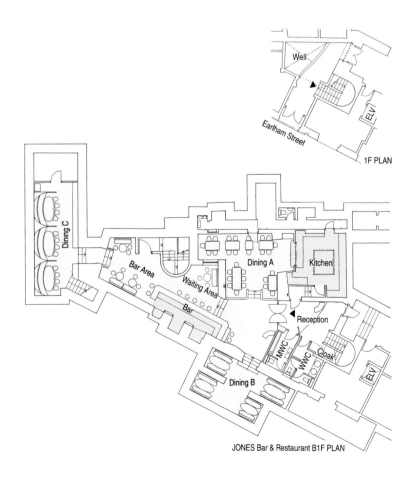

JONES Bar & Restaurant B1F PLAN

ソウルにできたアヴァンギャルドな雰囲気のバー

157 ステアズ

韓国，ソウル

Bar 157 STAIRS
363-6, Sukyo-Dong Mapo-Gu, Seoul, South Korea
Planner : Choi.Jung Hwa　　Designer : Kim.Dong-Jin
Sculptor : Jeon.Seong-Ho

1．道路側から見たアプローチ階段まわり。正面階段上部の右側が入り口　View of the approach stairs from the street

2

●ソリッドな襞で覆われた外部階段

韓国は、台湾、香港、シンガポールとともに、近年、経済の成長が目覚ましく、経済解放政策により急成長を遂げつつある中国の存在と相まって、アジアを世界で最も活気のある地域にしている。経済の成長は、生活のレベルを着実に上げ、建築を含めたデザインのレベルもそれに伴い上昇していく。韓国もその例外ではない。

首都・ソウルの中心街から5キロばかり離れた西側地区、新村の弘益大学ちかくにできたこのバーは、立地的な条件もあり、若い世代が集まる人気の店である。デザイン上の特徴は、店名の由来ともなっているアプローチの外部階段にある。1階の道路から2階の店内に至る階段は扇形に広がりながら上昇し、その一部は3階レベルにまで延びる。表面を覆うメタリックな布状のカバーはポリアクリル樹脂でコーティングされ、固められた表面を鉛色に塗られて、一見、ソリッドな金属のように見える。また、シンプルな内部空間を構成する唯一の要素であるカウンターも、表面が階段と同じ素材で仕上げられている。

オープン当時には、階段の手すりに男性の下半身裸像が林立していたが、現在は撤去されて、その姿を見ることはできない。

157 STAIRS
South Korea, together with Taiwan, Hong Kong, and Singapore, is making rapid progress in economy and it can be said that South Korea will play a leading role in above-mentioned countries, which can be also true of China that drastically pushes forward new economical order. Economic growth directly influences living standard and eventually change architectural design level. South Korea clearly exemplifies the process.

A bar opened in Sukyo-Dong, five kilometers west from the Seoul. A bar named 157 Stairs is in a good location and neighborhood and attracts many young people. As the name shows, characteristic design element is approach stairs going from the ground level to the second floor and to the third floor, extending like a shape of fan. It seems to be made of solid metal but it is just covered with metallic cloth cover coated with poly-acrylic resin. A bar counter, a focal point of simple interior, is made the same way.

When this bar opened, male naked lower parts objects were displayed on the handrail of the stairs, but later unfortunately they were removed.

Photos by Park. Hee Sung,
text by Choi Jung Hwa

2．アプローチ階段ディテール。ポリアクリル樹脂でコーティングされた布は鉛色の塗装によりソリッドな金属のように見える
3．店内奥の湾曲したバーカウンター。カウンタートップと腰は階段部と同じ素材で覆われている
4．道路側から見たカウンター正面全景
2．Details of the approach stairs coating by poly-acrylic resin
3．Details of the bar counter side using same material on the stairs
4．Whole view of the counter from the street side

3

4

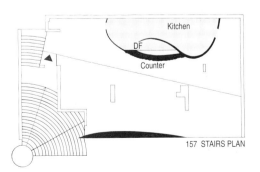

157 STAIRS PLAN

気分に応じた利用方法が選択できるトロントのナイトクラブ

オーキッド

カナダ，オンタリオ州，トロント

Nightclub ORCHID

Tront, Ontario, Canada
Designer : Yabu Pushelberg

1．入り口側から見たダンスフロアと立ち飲み用テーブル
2．店内中央のダンスフロアからメーンバー方向を見る。柱形のフォルムはオーキッド（蘭）の花芯の構造をイメージさせる
1．Whole view of the dance floor from the entry side
2．View from the dance floor to the main bar

1

2

3

●蘭とサラセニアからのイメージと発想
カナダ・トロントのファッション街から少し外れた位置にあるこのナイトクラブは、1000平方メートルを超える大型店でありながら、ヒューマンスケールで、客が気分に応じて利用の仕方を決めることが可能なように計画された。中央には気軽に踊れるフリー・ダンスエリアが設けられているが、同時に多くのアルコーブや親近感を感じさせる小スペースもあり、空間の用途がハッキリしすぎないようにデザイン面でも配慮されている。客はそれらの空間を漂いながら、語り合い、魚群のように空間を泳ぐ人を観察し、あるいは観察しあうことができる。
店内の中心部に林立する渦巻いたフォルムの柱は、店名である"オーキッド"（蘭）の雌雄の一体化したコラムナとよばれる中心構造体をイメージさせるものであり、他にも、カーブリニア（曲線）様式、ビオモルフィズム（生物形態／観）などが、ライ

トモチーフとしてインテリアのあちこちで繰り返し使用されている。シンプルでオーガニックなディテールは植物の内部、とりわけ花芯の周囲を思わせ、蘭より単純な構造だが、どことなく似ている食虫植物・サラセニアの、開いた口に取り込まれる獲物のように客を内部に引きつける魅力を持っている。

ORCHID
Little bit far from busy streets in Toronto, a night club Orchid became a fashionable hot spot, despite of its big scale of more than 1000 square meters, as the interior is designed for customers to feel comfortable, not over-whelmed by the scale. The interior is consisted of the central free dance area, and small rooms with alcoves, etc. Most areas are gently curved and flexible. Customers, like rambling fish, pass though crowd randomly seeing others passing here and there.

Organic columns in the main area appeared to be designed upon a image of columna of a flowers of orchid. Curve linear lines and biomorphism details are instinctively make us think of the inner part of a flower of orchid, particularly stigma and other parts related to reproduction. This club has charm to attract people as a carnivorous plant catching insects with its lid of a honey pitcher open or with its velvet-like lamina spread.

Text by Masaaki Takahashi

3．店内奥右側のVIPラウンジを休憩スペース側から見る
4．奥左側のトイレ前に設けられた休憩スペース
3．View of VIP lounge from the resting space side
4．View of the resting space in front of the toilet

4

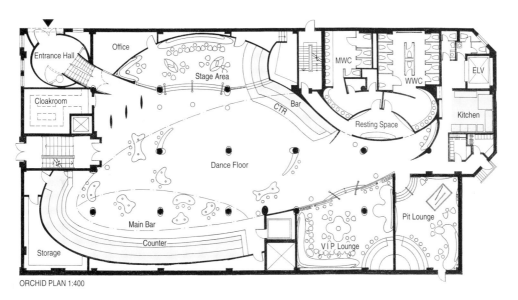

ORCHID PLAN 1:400

倉庫の中地下を改装したトロントのディスコクラブ

スティライフ
カナダ，トロント

Nightclub STILIFE
John Street, Tront, Ontario, Canada
Designer : Yabu Pushelberg

1．ダンスフロアに面したバーカウンターを入り口側から見る。腰のパターンは
　　原始部族の絵文字をイメージしたもの
2．ダンスフロアとスタンディング・カウンターを仕切るチェーン・スクリーン
1．Whole view of the bar counter from the gate side
2．View of the chain screen dividing the dance floor and standing counter

3

4

3. 店内左奥のラウンジエリア。プリミティブなデザインが床・壁・ベンチシートに展開されている
4. ラウンジエリアのリップチェア
5. ダンスフロア側からゲートを通してエントランスホール壁面のウォータースカルプチャーを見る。気泡の動きにより様々な表情を見せる
3. View of the bench seat and wall sculpture in the lounge area
4. Details of the lip chair in the lounge area
5. View of the water sculpture through the gate from the dance floor

●原始とモダンの対比がデザインのテーマ

カナダは，ヨーロッパの移民が中心になって建国
されて以来，120年という浅い歴史のために，国
としてのデザイン的な特徴をイメージとして思い
浮かべるのが難しい。やはりデザインも，国とし
ての歴史や伝統，民族性といった文化的背景に負
うところが大きいのである。しかし，近年になっ
て，商業的な中心といえるトロントをホームグラ
ウンドに，歴史の浅さを逆手に取り，何ものにも
とらわれない自由さで，新しいカナダデザインの
アイデンティティーを確立しようという動きが活
発になってきた。このナイトクラブのデザインも
そのようなムーブメントの一つとしてとらえるこ
とができよう。

トロントの中心部にできたこのディスコクラブは，
倉庫の中地下を改装したもので，約700平方メー
トルの面積を持つ。店内は中央のオープンなダン
ススペースと，ラウンジスペースに二分され，ダ
ンススペースの周囲にはシートエリアやバーエリ
アが配されている。

デザインのテーマは，ヨーロッパのアートムーブ
メントと原始部族の楯や絵文字，あるいは未加工
の素材とハイテクノロジーという対比的な存在を
組み合わせることであった。例えば，バーカウン
ターの腰を構成するモザイクタイルのパターンは
原始的な絵文字を模したもので，それをメカニカ
ルなライトパターンが照らし出しているといった
具合であり，このような対比の手法が空間を，よ
り魅力的なものにしている。

STILIFE

It may be said that imaging the face of
Canada is quite difficult, for it has just about
120 years history of immigration and has
various cultural and geographical aspects. So,
Canadian design may reflect the complicated
national character. In these years, designers
are more expressive in their style, based
mostly upon Toronto and Motreal. Their style
is free from anything, making use of youth
cultural identity to establish Canadian style. A
night club Stilife is a good example of such
movement. This club was renovated from a
half basement of a warehouse and the total
floor area is 700 square meters. The interior is
divided into two areas : the central dance area
and lounge area. Around the dance area,
there are seats and a bar. The design theme
is European art movements and primitive art
motif such as forms of shields and pictorial
symbols. In other words, it is to combine low-
tech materials with high technology. Mosaic
pattern of a bar counter, for example, is from
a primitive art hieroglyph, and the counter is lit
up by mechanical lighting. The contrast is
attractive.

Photos by David Whitaker

5

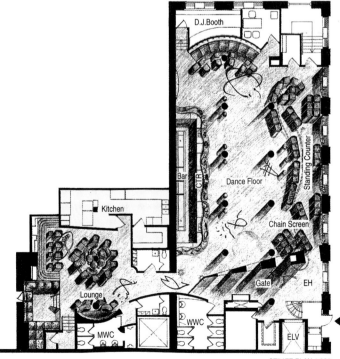

STILIFE PLAN 1:300

サソリをシンボルとしたトロントの未来的ディスコクラブ

スコーピオ

カナダ，トロント

Nightclub SKORPIO

17A Yorkville Avenue, Toront, Ontario, Canada
Designer : Alexandre and Gregory Gatserelia

1．店内奥右側にあるＶＩＰルームをダンスフロア奥のバー側から見る。仕切りスクリーン上部に突き出した
　　メタルの突起はサソリの尻尾をイメージ
2．入り口側バー席からダンスフロアに面したソファ席を見る。ソファの背もサソリの尻尾を意匠化している
1．View of the VIP room from the dance floor side
2．View from the entry side to the sofa seatings

1

3

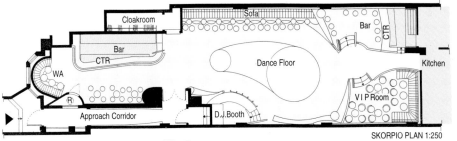

SKORPIO PLAN 1:250

Cloakroom
Sofa
Bar
CTR
Bar
CTR
Dance Floor
Kitchen
WA
R
VIP Room
Approach Corridor
D.J. Booth

●1930年代にイメージされた未来空間

トロントでも流行の先端を行く街・ヨークビル
も、西のはずれまで行くと地味な町並みになり、
夜は通行人も多くない寂しい通りとなる。通り
に面したレンガ造りのビル1階にできたこのディ
スコクラブは、オーナーの"未来的なイメー
ジを持った、センセーショナルでドラマチック
なクラブを"という要望を満たすことが計画の
出発点となった。

結果として、デザインのコンセプトはジュー
ル・ベルヌ的で、1930年代にイメージされた未
来空間を連想させるものとなった。それは、小
説・海底2万マイルの主人公・ネモ船長や、ベ
ルヌ好みの巨大化した昆虫などのイメージをふ
くらませたものである。ダンスフロアのある中
央のメーン空間は、ネモ船長の船室であり、ス
チール、ガラス、和紙などで店名でもあるサソ
リのディテールがアレンジされている。地階の
イメージは"海底の夢"。壁や柱に用いられてい
るガラス玉はまるで気泡のように見え、ビロー
ドのカーペットや天井なども海の色にされてい
る。また、地階中央のソファは女性の脚をシュ
ールな感覚で表現している。

SKORPIO

The west edge of fashionable ritzy Yorkville
looks quite subdued and is seemingly a
nothing-happens-area. But, there is something exciting behind ordinary street scene.
Skorpio is created upon owner's plan to set up
a futuristic, sensational, and dramatic club
here. Designer chose theme from Jules
Verne's novel "Twenty Thousand League
Under the Sea" and they express it in futuristic architectural style of 1930s. The main
dance room is upon images of an enigmatic
Capt. Nemo's room, and Verne's images of
gigantic insects are express by scorpions
made of steel, glass, papers, etc. The
basement is designs as a "dream of the sea
bed". Glass balls are like bubbles, velvet
carpet and ceiling are sea colors. Impressive
surrealistic design element is a leg of a sofa
like a woman's leg made of steel.

Photos by Rico Bela,
text by Masaaki Takahashi

4

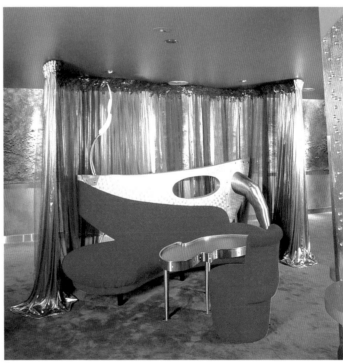

5

3．右奥のVIPルームから見たダンスフロア全景
4．"海底の夢"をテーマに海の色で統一された地下1階のラウンジ空間
5．地下1階ラウンジの中央に置かれたシュールなデザインのソファ。背当てから
　金属製の女性の脚が生えている
3．Whole view of the dance floor from the VIP room
4．View of the seatings in the lounge(B1F)
5．View of the sofa in the lounge(B1F)

ワンダーランドのようなトロント郊外のディスコクラブ

アムネジア

カナダ，トロント

Nightclub AMNESIA

177 Whitemore Ave. Hwy 7 Weston Rd, Ontario, Canada
Designer : II by IV Dan Menchions, Keith Rushbrook

1．1階入り口ホールから見たキャッシャーブース。左右が店内への入り
　　口扉
2．1階中央のダンスフロアを2階ラウンジバーから階段部を通して見る
1．View of the ticket booth from the entry side
2．View of the dance floor from the second floor

1

2

3

●万華鏡パターンが創りだす別世界
トロントの郊外、車で1時間弱の場所にできたこのディスコクラブは、もともとはタイル会社のショールームを兼ねた倉庫であり、1400平方メートルの広さを持つ。店名の"アムネジア"は記憶喪失という意味であり、この店にきて日常生活のストレスを忘れ、解放された気分で、笑いと気晴らしの世界に浸れる別世界を提供しようというショップ・コンセプトから選ばれた。
L字形の敷地を生かして、内部はメーンのクラブエリアとカフェ・ラウンジに効率的に二分され、その間を仕切るドアはクラブが終わると閉められるが、通り側からの別の入り口から出入りすることができる。地味な外観とはうらはらに、入り口と内部を結ぶチケット売り場のホワイエは、まるで大人のためのワンダーランド。次に続くグラン

ドロビーのカレードスコープ（万華鏡）を思わせる、楽しく、華やかな空間を予見させるに十分なデザインである。このカレードスコープ・パターンと幾何学的な模様は、クラブエリアのメーン部分でも使われ、意匠上の大きな特徴となっている。左奥に突き出した形のカフェ・ラウンジは、鉄板サビ仕上げの壁面とビロード張りの家具が渋い雰囲気を醸し出し、ポップなクラブエリアとは異なった空間に仕上がっている。

AMNESIA
Renovated from a tile company's warehouse and showroom, Amnesia is a 1,400 square meters large club in a suburb of Toronto. The

design concept is, as the name suggests, to create a wonderland where people divert themselves as amnesias from biting reality.
Making use of L-shaped site, Amnesia is consisted of the main club area and cafe bar lounge, which can be partitioned and have each entrance. The outside is unnoticed but the interior is dazzlingly colorful. The foyer is the threshold to the wonderland and the lively grand lobby is like the inside of kaleidoscope. Jellybean color scheme and kaleidoscope-geometric pattern are widely used in the interior. The cafe lounge is subdued and looks different from the club area, with rusted iron walls and velvet-covered furniture.

Photos by David Whitaker,
text by Masaaki Takahashi

3． 2階ラウンジバーから吹き抜けを通して下部の
　　グランドロビーを見る。"めまい"を感じさせる
　　万華鏡のような色使い
4． ダンスフロアに面した壁面にアルコーブのよう
　　に穿たれたカクテルラウンジの出入り口
5． カクテルラウンジの内部空間
3． Down view from the second floor to the
　　grand robby through the well
4． Entrance view of the cocktail lounge from
　　the dance floor side
5． Interior view of the cocktail lounge

6

7

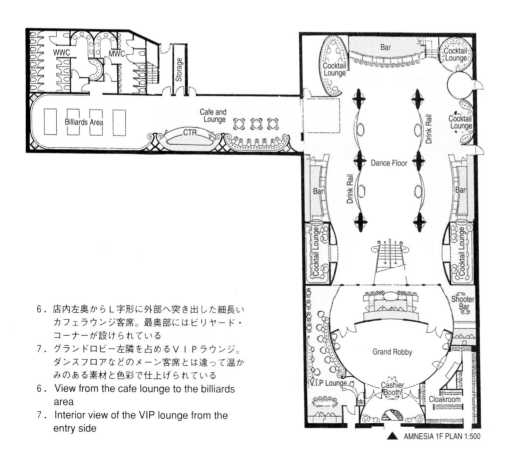

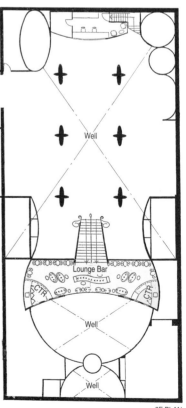

6．店内左奥からＬ字形に外部へ突き出した細長い
カフェラウンジ客席。最奥部にはビリヤード・
コーナーが設けられている
7．グランドロビー左隣を占めるＶＩＰラウンジ。
ダンスフロアなどのメーン客席とは違って温か
みのある素材と色彩で仕上げられている
6．View from the cafe lounge to the billiards
area
7．Interior view of the VIP lounge from the
entry side

▲ AMNESIA 1F PLAN 1:500

2F PLAN

エーゲ海の雰囲気をトロントに再現したナイトクラブ

オーパ

カナダ，トロント

Nightclub OPA

435 Danforth Ave, Subterranean Level, Tront, Ontario, Canada
Designer : II by IV Dan Menchions, Keith Rushbrook

1

１．ダンスフロアに面したソファ席。背当てにはギリシャ特有のメ
　アンダー・パターンが配されている
２．店内左側を占めるラウンジエリアをD.J.ブース前から入り口方
　向へ見る
１．View of the sofa seatings from the dance floor
２．View from the lounge area to the entry side

2

●ギリシャを表現するメアンダー・パターン

トロントの、レストランが多いダンフォース・ストリートにできた小型のディスコ的なナイトクラブ。この店のコンセプトは、ギリシャのエーゲ海に浮かぶ風光明媚で豊かな自然を持つナクソス島から採られた。ちなみに"オーバ"という言葉は、闘牛の掛け声などで使われる"オーレ"というスペイン語があるが、それと同じ意味のギリシャ語を指す。

設計に際しては、ギリシャの男性立像がイメージとして選ばれ、これにギリシャ特有の鍵模様（キー・パターン）の一つである"メアンダー"とよばれるデザインパターンが具体的に用いられた。メアンダーとは、蛇行しながらエーゲ海に注ぐトルコ側に面した川の名前に由来するパターンである。色彩も、島の雰囲気を再現するため、壁の色は砂を表す黄色、床と家具には海の色のグラデーションとしてターコイズ・ブルーとパープルが使われている。

店内の中心部を占めるのは、長いカウンターを持つバーエリアで、右端部分には陶片とガラスで覆われた直線的なラセンの塔状彫刻が配されている。カウンターのトップは彫刻と同じ素材で覆われており、側面と腰部分にはそれぞれメアンダーのパターンが施され、立ち飲みウンターの支持フレームや、イスの張り地に施された同じパターンと照応している。

OPA

Opa is among nice restaurants standing side by side on Danforth Avenue in Toronto. This small night club is designed upon a theme of picturesque Naxos island in the Aegean Sea. Opa means a Greek shout like Ole in Spanish. Classical Greek figure sculptures and Greek key pattern are major leit-motifs. Also meander pattern is applied from images of River Meander winding and flowing in the Aegean Sea.

Color scheme represents an atmosphere of the Greek island, like sand yellow for walls, and turquoise blue, as colors of gradated sea blue, for floor and furniture.

A bar area with a long counter is the center of the interior. A pole like sculpture is installed on the corner covered with fragments of glass and ceramics. Greek key patterns are also used on sides of the counter, and seating covers of chairs.

Photos by David Whitaker,
text by Masaaki Takahashi

3．ダンスフロアから見たバーカウンター全景。右端に"砂の彫刻"を持つ。カウンタートップの側面と腰、スツールの座など、あらゆるところにメアンダー・パターンが繰り返し使われている
3．Whole view of the bar counter from the dance floor

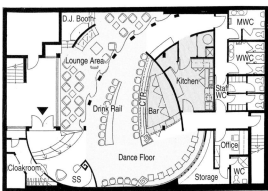

OPA PLAN 1:200

3

コミックスをテーマにしたフィレンツェのバー＆レストラン

ベティ・ブープ

イタリア，フィレンツェ

Bar & Restaurant BETTY BOOP

26r, Via Degli Alfani, Firenze, Italia
Designer : Giuseppe Di Somma

１．入り口に面した"ドナルド・ダックの三人の甥に捧げる部屋"から奥方向を見る
２．入り口から二番目にある"異なったイスの部屋"。21人の若いデザイナーの作品
　　が所狭しと並んでいる
１．View of the counter table in the room "three nephews of Donald Duck"
２．View of the room with various chairs from the Camelot room

1

2

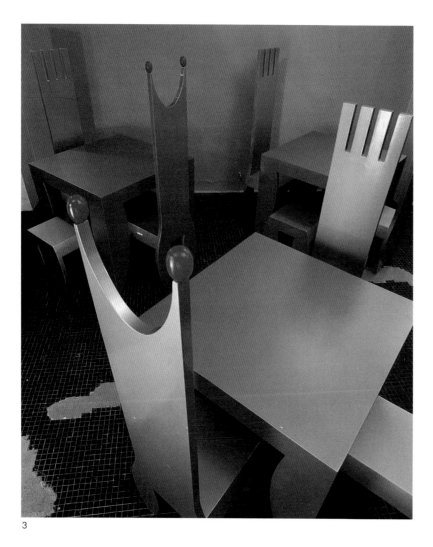

3

3．入り口から三番目の"キャメロットの部屋"に置かれた金色のテーブルとイス
4．彩色された平面図
3．Details of furniture in the Camelot room
4．Coloring plan

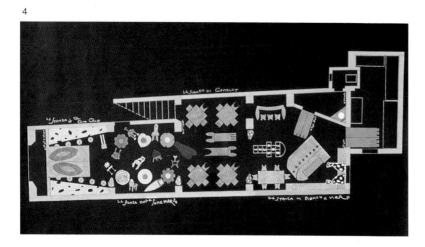

4

●21人のデザインしたイスが並ぶ空間

イタリア中部の都市・フィレンツェは、ローマと並ぶ古い歴史を持つ街で、中世には都市国家としてメディチ家の支配のもとに繁栄し、イタリア・ルネサンスの中心地として、レオナルド・ダ・ビンチなどの世界的に有名な作品や建築物が今も多く残されている。この伝統を引き継いでか、現代においても美術だけでなく建築やデザインの活動も盛んで、1960年代から1970年代にかけては"ラディカル・アーキテクチュア"とよばれるデザイン・ムーブメントを生み、アーキ・ズーム、スーパー・ステュディオなどのグループを輩出した。しかし、人口約40万と都市としての規模が小さいため、実際的な活動拠点を少し離れた工業都市・ミラノに移さざるを得ないケースがほとんどである。このレストラン＆バーは、フィレンツェで活動を開始し、現在ではミラノで活躍中の若い設計者が地元に残した作品の一つである。店のデザインテーマは、店名から分かるとおり初期のコミックスおよびアニメーションのキャラクターである。約80平方メートルの面積を持つ店内は、入り口から順に奥へ、ドナルド・ダックの三人の甥に捧げる部屋、異なったイスの部屋、キャメロットの部屋、白と黒の部屋の四つの部分からなる。特に面白いのは異なったイスの部屋で、そこにはフィレンツェの若いデザイナー21人の作ったイスが所狭しと置かれている。

BETTY BOOP

Florence is a cultural and intellectual center of Italy from Middle Ages. It was virtually ruled and flourished by Medici family in the 15th century and produced numerous master pieces of art and architecture of the Renaissance like Leonard da Vinci, etc. Today new types of art, architecture, and design still hatch in this city. In 1960s and 1970s, "Radical Architecture" movement was born and architects groups like Archi Zoom and Super Studio appeared. They are, however, usually have to move to an industrial city like Milano, because the scale of Florence is quite small with only population 400,000.
Betty Boop is a project designed by a young designer who started his career in Florence and now works in Milano. The interior design theme is, as in its name, an old cartoon characters. The floor site is about 80 square meters. There are a room dedicated for three nephews of Donald Duck, a room with various chairs, a Camelot room, and a black and white room. Above all the second room is interesting, crowded with chairs and chairs by twenty one different designers.

Photos by Alberto Petra

ヤングの人気を集めるマドリードのシンプルなディスコバー

ハノイ

スペイン，マドリード

Disco-bar HANOI

Hortaleza 81, Madrid, Spain
Designer : Javier de Calzada

1．ウエーティングエリアから見たセンターホール。右側にD.J.ブースが見える　View of the center hall from the waiting area

●鰻の寝床状の細長い平面を巧みに利用する
スペインの首都・マドリッドの夜は遅い。同じラ
テン系のイタリアとともに、スペインも楽しみの
ためにエネルギーを費やすのを厭わないのが国民
性なのである。午前2時、3時になってもバーや
ディスコは混雑し、夜中にラッシュアワーがある
ほどである。そのせいであろうか、ブティックな
どのファッション関連に比較して飲食店が充実し
ているマドリッドでも、このディスコバーは若者
に人気の高い店である。
この店の特徴は、間口が6メートルと狭いわりに
奥行きが40メートルもある細長い平面形状を、巧
みに利用していることにある。六つのゾーンに分
けられた内部は、道路に面したエントランスホー
ル、カウンターのあるバーゾーン、多少座ること
のできるパブリックゾーン、ダンスホールのある

ゾーン、そしてガラスで仕切られたダイニングエ
リアと続き、最奥部が厨房という構成である。イ
ンテリアの仕上げ材は、床と壁がトラバーチンで、
水平に太い目地を入れることによって、奥行きの
長さをより強調している。天井は床・壁と同じベ
ージュで塗装されているが、ダンスホールの上部
だけは赤色に塗られた折り上げの高天井とされ、
空間のアクセントの役割を果たしている。

HANOI
People in Madrid love to enjoy long night life,
as most Europeans do. Particularly in Spain, it
seems to me, people energetically entertain
themselves as possible as they can. Even
after two or three a.m., bars are crowded like
traffic jam. Compared with boutiques and
other shops, bars, cafes, and restaurants are

more and of high quality. Under these
circumstances, Hanoi is very popular for
youngsters. The site of this disco-bar is
characteristically long and narrow. The width
is six meters and the depth is 40 meters.
Making most of the length, the interior is
effectively divided into six areas;entrance hall,
counter bar area, open area with some seats,
dance hall, dining area with glazed partitions,
and the kitchen. Travertin is used for floor and
wall on which bald stripes goes strikingly to
emphasizes the interior depth. The ceiling is
painted beige as floor and walls, and the
coved ceiling of the dance hall is red, an
accentuated interior color.

Photos by Yoichi Horimoto,
text by Masaatsu Fukazawa

3

4

2．奥のダンスフロアをセンターホール側から見る。左手にダイニングエリア、
　　右手にバーカウンターが見える
3．ガラスで仕切られたダイニングエリア内部から見たダンスフロア
4．店内最奥部を占めるダイニングエリア内部客席
2．View of the dance floor to the dining area
3．View from the dining area to the dance floor
4．Interior view of the dining area

2

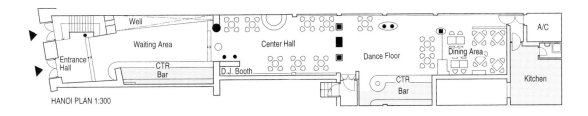

HANOI PLAN 1:300

リスボンのウオーターフロントにできたディスコ&バー

キャピタル

ポルトガル，リスボン

Disco Bar KAPITAL
Avend 24 de Julho 68, 1200 Lisboa, Portugal
Designer : Salavisa

1

1．エントランスホール右手の階段。2・3階バーへのアプローチ階段となっている
2．エントランスホールから正面のディスコ入り口扉方向を見る
3．ディスコ入り口左側のカウンター席。右側には巨大な鉄仮面のオブジェが配され、
　　カウンターバックのシロッコファンは機能と意匠を兼ねている
1．View to the disco entry from the entrance hall(1F)
2．View of the staircase in the entrance hall to the second floor(1F)
3．View of the disco counter from the entry side(1F)

2

●スケールアウトされた古典的エレメント
ポルトガルの首都・リスボンは、大西洋に注ぐテージョ川を少し遡った河口部に位置する。中心街の南側にあるコメルシオ広場から西へ行くと、そこは開発が進んでいるウォーターフロント地区で、かつては港湾倉庫の立ち並ぶ殺伐とした風景が続いていた。しかし、現在では幾つものディスコができ、夏期の週末ともなると若者の車で一杯になり、時には2万人以上の人々が集まる。元倉庫を改装したこのディスコ&バーは、比較的新しいナイトスポットで、営業時間が深夜の0時30分から朝の4時まで。タキシードやドレスを着たカップルも多く、客層もかなりアッパークラスを対象と

しているが、週末には4000人近い客が集まるとのことである。
店内の構成は、1階エントランスホールをはいった正面がディスコの入り口ドア。内部へ進むと奥正面に巨大な鉄の仮面が鎮座し、不気味な雰囲気を漂わせている。エントランスホール右手の大きな階段から直接にアプローチする2階のバーは、長い8の字形のカウンターが中心で、交差する部分の甲板がうねるように、もう一方の甲板を跨いだデザインがポイントである。2階バーから階段を上がった3階屋上もバーであるが、三方が開け放たれ、海の潮風が吹き抜けて、解放的な気分にさせてくれるスペースとなっている。

KAPITAL
Situated at the mouth of River Tejo flowing into the Atlantic Ocean, Lisbon is expanding its waterfront redevelopment projects in the west area from Praca do Comercio in the south of the city. The area looks desolated with warehouses. Recently, however, a number of discos opened in this area and a streets are full of cars of young people every weekends during summer. Sometimes the area is overcrowded with more than 20,000 people. Kapital, renovated from a warehouse, is one of new comers here, and the open hour is from 12:30 a.m. to 4:00 a.m. Some customers are dressed in dinner jackets or evening dresses,

4

5

6

as the target customers covers upper class. Some 4,000 people drop in Kapital on the weekend. Going through the entrance hall on the first floor, you find the door to the disco. In the back, you also find a queer object, a huge iron mask. A bar on the second floor is accessed by big stairs on the right side of the entrance hall. The bar has a double ovals-shaped counter of two panels, the counter cross showing beautiful wavy lines and rolling over form. If you go up further to the rooftop, you again come across another bar with three openings and then sea breeze comforts you.

Photos by Yoichi Horimoto, text by Masaatsu Fukazawa

4．2階バーエリアの中央に配された8の字形の長大なカウンターを3階への階段上部から見る
5．船の舳先のようにダイナミックに延びる2階バーエリアの天井化粧梁形
6．古典的な建築エレメントをスケールアウトした2階バーエリアの巨大な渦巻装飾
4．View of the long counter from the stairs in the bar area(2F)
5．View of the beam and counter in the bar area(2F)
6．View of the big volute under the beam in bar area(2F)

アナーキーな雰囲気の漂うブリュッセルのディスコ

ノボ

ベルギー，ブリュッセル

Disco NOBO
10 Rue du Marche aux Herbes, Brussel, Belgium
Designer : Stijn

1．入り口側のロングテーブル席からカウンター席方向を見る。上部に見
　える中2階部分はアートギャラリーとなる
2．入り口側から見た店内へのゲートと中2階への階段まわり。布で覆わ
　れた入り口空間がこの店の閉鎖的な性格を象徴している
1．View from the long table to the bar counter
2．View of the entrance gate and stairs to the mezzanine

2

1

●外界から隔絶されたローテック空間
　EC統合に向けての思惑と，それに伴う建設ラッ
シュが進むブリュッセルの街の雰囲気を拒絶するかの
ように，ガレージを改装したこのディスコは無表情に
建っている。営業時間は午後11時から明け方まで。5
人の若者が共同経営しており，金曜日と土曜日の週2
日しか開いていないが，多くのヤングが他の都市から
も集まってくるアナーキーな魅力を持った空間である。

内部は電動ノコギリで切断したままの生木、荷造り用のロープ、さびた鉄板とパイプ、イミテーションの骨など、ローテックな素材が充満し、それらを赤、青、黄色などのカラースポットが浮かび上がらせる。世の中のデザイン的な動向とは無関係な率直さとオリジナリティーで、アンチでアナーキーな独自の世界を造り上げたこの店は、改装中の中2階をアートギャラリーにする予定である。

NOBO

Against an active and positive air of Brussels which has a building boom towards the final stage of EU unification, this disco Nobo stands bluntly. Open hour is from eleven a.m. to dawn. Punckish charm of Nobo attracts many young customers from different cities. Raw lumbers cut roughly by a chain-saw, industrial packing ropes, rusted iron plates and pipes, fake bones, and other anarchic mishmash decorates the interior and they are lit up by colorful lighting such as yellow, red, blue, and so on. Unique, stark, and indifferent to so-called design trend of the world, this disco produces an environment for anti-establishment. The mezzanine is going to become an art gallery, by the way.

Photos and text by Yoichi Horimoto

3. 中2階レベルから下部のロングテーブル席方向を見る。左上のステージはガレージの既存リフトスペースを利用したもの
View to the long table from the mezzanine level

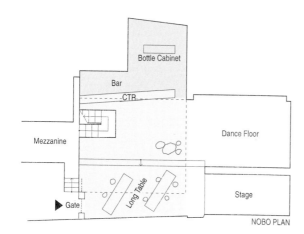

バルセロナ郊外にある海浜リゾート施設の核となるディスコ

パーチャ

スペイン，タラゴナ

Discotheque PACHA

Pineda Beach, Vila-sega(Tarragona), Spain
Architect : Juli Capella, Quim Larrea, Jaume Castellvi

1

1．ディスコを取り巻く外部テラス席から見たタワーの外観。
　周囲にはこのほかレストラン棟なども配されている
2．駐車場側から見た外観夜景。ネオンに縁取られたタワーは
　ランドマークの役割を果たしている
1．Night view of the tower from the outside terrace
2．Night view of the facade from the parking area

2

3

3. 1階左側入り口から見た受付＆レジカウンターまわり。左右の階段を上がると2階サテライトバーへ至る
4. 1階右奥の"大地のバー"側から見たダンスフロア。左奥に"火のバー"、右奥に"大気のバー"が見える
3. View of the reception counter from the entry
4. Whole view of the dance floor from the earth bar side

4

5

6

7

●地球を構成する四つのエレメントを表現

バルセロナの南西約100キロメートルにあるピネダ・ビーチにできたこのディスコは、海浜リゾート施設の核として建設され、周囲にはスイミングプールやレストラン、各種のバーなどを付帯施設として持っている。建物の端部には高いタワーが設けられ、展望台としての役割の他に、夜間は赤いネオンにふちどられて一目で分かるシンボル的なサインとしての機能を果たしている。アフターダンスには、客は展望台に登り、周囲のパノラミックな景観を楽しみながら、別世界のムードに浸ることができるという、いかにもリゾート地らしい設定のディスコである。内部空間はダンスフロアのある1階がメーンで、その上部にある中2階的なフロアはバルコニー状になっており、その両端にサテライト・バーと星の形をしたバーとが設けられている。デザインのコンセプトは、神話の世界や古典的自然観にみられる、地球を構成する四つのエレメント、すなわち、水、大地、大気、火をシンボリックに表現したものである。まず"水"は、1階中央の半透明ガラスブロックでできたダンスフロア。その下部は水の満たされたプールで、人々は水の上でダンスを踊ることになる。あとの三つは、ダンスフロアを取り巻く"大地のバー"、"大気のバー"、"火のバー"の三つにそれぞれデザインテーマとして反映されている。

PACHA

Pacha is on Pineda Beach, Tarragona, some100 kilometers southwest of Barcelona. This disco is the core of a beach resort center covering a swimming pool, restaurants, and various bars. A high observatory is built on the edge of the site. The tower, rimmed by red neon lamps, makes an icon of the resort facility at night. So, in this resort type disco, you can enjoy dancing and looking a panoramic view. The main area is a dance hall on the first floor and a mezzanine-like balcony above it. The design concept is the four elements ; water, earth, wind and fire. "The water element" is expressed in the central dance hall with translucent glass blocks, so people dance on the water. Other three elements are represented in design of three bars.

5．1階右側"大地のバー"わきから見たダンスフロアと"火のバー"。半透明ガラスブロックのダンスフロア床面下側は水が満たされたプールとなっている
6．石積みの壁面とカウンターで構成された右奥の"大地のバー"
7．1階右側入り口わきの女性用トイレ内部
8．レーザー光線に浮き上がるダンスフロア。ディスコには珍しく正面奥に広いガラス面の開口部が取られている

5．View of the dance floor and the fire bar from the earth bar side
6．View of the earth bar
7．Interior view of woman's toilet
8．View of the dance floor from the fire bar to the stage

8

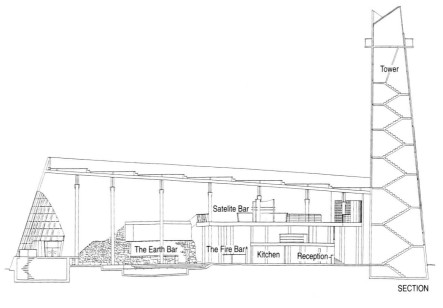

SECTION

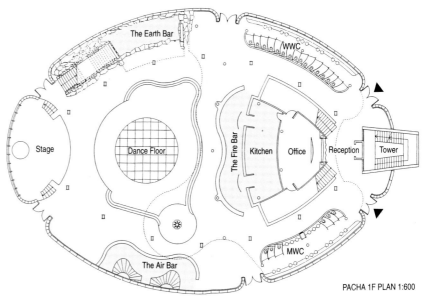

PACHA 1F PLAN 1:600

バルセロナにできたメカニカルな形態のメガ・ディスコ&ナイトクラブ

グラン・ベルベット

スペイン，バルセロナ

Nightclub & Disco GRAN VELVET

Poligono Montigala, Badalona, Barcelona,Spain
Architect : Alfred Arribas, Miguel Morte

1. 地下１階左奥のメディカル・ルーム側から階段
   下空間を通してバー方向を見る。上部に１階D.J.
   ブースと２階プライベートバーの円盤状底部が
   見える
1. View of the stairwell and bar area from the
   medical room side(B1F)

2

2．ダンスフロア上部の吹き抜けに張り出した2階円形プライベートバー
　　の内部空間。1987年につくられたバー・ベルベットの空間が忠実に再
　　現されている
3．地下1階のダンスフロアをスロープ階段の上がり口から見る。手前の
　　円形ステージは油圧シリンダーにより昇降し，1階レベルまで上げる
　　ことができる
4．1階入り口に面したチケットカウンター

2．Interior view of the private bar(2F)
3．View of the dance floor and stage from the slope stairs bottom
　　(B1F)
4．View of the ticket counter(1F)

3

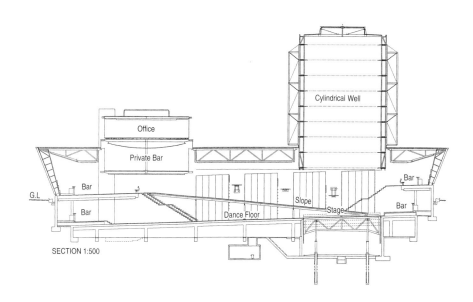

SECTION 1:500

4

5. 建築を垂直に貫く円筒形の吹き抜け頂部に設けられた羽根形のオブジェ
View of the art object in the cylindrical well from the stage

●エアロダイナミクスを基本とした発想

世界を沸かせたバルセロナ・オリンピック。その翌年に，建築面積約1500平方メートルのこのメガディスコ＆ナイトクラブは，同じ建築家が1988年につくった同名のナイトクラブの新築リニューアルとしてオープンした。店名が同じとはいえ，構造，規模，コンセプトがあまりにもかけ離れているため，連続性はなく，むしろ1987年に同じ建築家が手掛けた"バー・ベルベット"のコンセプトを発展させたプロジェクトといえる。

外観と内部空間を特徴づけているのは，巨大な3層吹き抜けを突き抜け，さらに屋上レベルから外部へと突き出したシリンダー状のタワーである。タワーの頂部には，シロッコファンをイメージさせるオブジェが取り付けられ，エアロダイナミクスを基本とした発想が表現されている。内部のメーンフロアは，1階入り口ホールから吹き抜けを斜めに貫く長さ約30メートルのスロープ・ブリッジを降りた地下1階で，ここにダンスフロアがある。

タワーの下部に当たるダンスフロア部分には，タワーと同じ平面形状の円形ステージが配され，地下1階と1階の床レベルのあいだを上下に昇降することができる。また，吹き抜けに半分張り出した形で，2階のレベルには円形のプライベート・バーが設けられ，そのインテリアは"バー・ベルベット"の空間を忠実に再現したものとなっている。

GRAN VELVET

The next year of exciting Barcelona Olympic, a gigantic night club and disco of 1,500 square meters building area reopened after the renovation by the original designer. It is Gran Velvet. Although the name remains, the renewed one is completely different from old one built in 1988, regarding its construction, scale, and design concept. In this project, the original concept is fully developed by the architect. A cylindrical tower goes through a huge three floor level open ceiling and juts out the roof. A sirrocco fan-shaped element mounts the top of the tower proclaiming designer's aerodynamics idea. The main area of the interior is a dance hall in the basement level with a 30 meters sloped bridge diagona-lly crossing the open ceiling. The dance hall has a round stage which can elevate up and down towards the ground floor. In the well, there is also a projected small bar whose interior is exactly reproduced from the original "Bar Velvet".

Photos by Domi Mora, text by Alfred Arribas

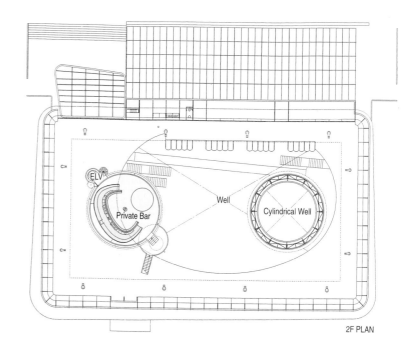

2F PLAN

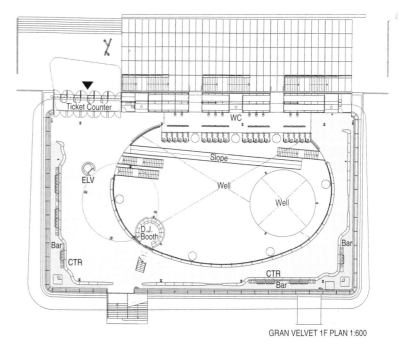

GRAN VELVET 1F PLAN 1:600

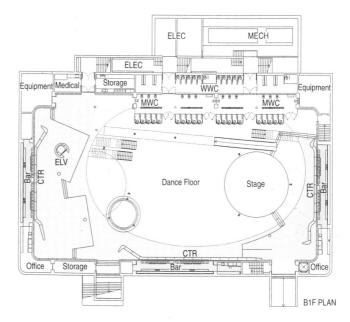

B1F PLAN